The Lavender Book

THE
LAVENDER BOOK

Margaret Roberts

PHOTOGRAPHY BY PHYLLIS GREEN

BRIZA

Published by

BRIZA PUBLICATIONS
CK 90/11690/23

PO Box 56569
Arcadia 0007
Pretoria
South Africa

First edition, first impression, 2004
First edition, second impression, 2006

ISBN 1 875093 38 9

Managing editor: Reneé Ferreira
Design and layout: Alicia Arntzen, The Purple Turtle Publishing Services
Cover design: Sally Whines, the Departure Lounge
Reproduction: Unifoto, Cape Town
Printed and bound by Tien Wah Press (Pte.) Ltd, Singapore

Contents

Lavandula dentata *'Elegans'* – *five-year-old bushes.*

Acknowledgements

The establishment of the Lavender Collection, the Lavender Register, at the Herbal Centre has been gradual – it began in 1985.

The first lavender to be grown here, was my Grandmother's lavender, followed by the old-fashioned green-leafed French lavender and then by the Hedge lavender, *Lavandula spica*, both brought in by obscure cuttings I took from friends' gardens in the Cape. An American visitor brought the grey

Lavandula dentata var. *candicans* as a single cutting, and a visitor from Holland in 1988 brought the tough and remarkable Dutch lavender, again as a single cutting.

Around 1989 my long-time friend Shaun Schurinck came to work in the newly established Herbal Centre nursery for just one or two days a week. She began her interest in the lavenders immediately and together we put together observations and notes on our first trial plantings and our shared fascination with lavender. Our excitement was tangible with our first imported cuttings from England in the spring of 1989. We talked lavender from morning until night and made careful notes, specially on our newly selected cuttings from the all-year-round flowering English lavender which came to South Africa as an *angustifolia* in about 1980. We chose cuttings from the biggest and most vigorous bushes. This is how we, Shaun and I, and the nursery staff, established one of the best lavenders in South Africa, now known as *Lavandula intermedia* 'Margaret Roberts' in the nursery trade.

I dedicate this book to my precious friend Shaun, who died in May 2001, with so much gratitude that we could share the lavender passion and the lavender experience, that we stoked the lavender fires in this great land of ours, and that the lavender trials continue with ever increasing new varieties – not just the 15 to 20 lavenders she worked on, but more and more each year. We know she walks with us, she watches over the lavenders and she rejoices with us that her daughter, Karen, who works now in her place in the nursery, walks in her footsteps and is developing the lavender passion just like her mother.

Thank you to all the staff at the Herbal Centre, the gardens, the nursery and the studio staff. Each and every one plays an enormous role in our lavender production, in our yearly spring lavender festivals and our handmade lavender products in the shop.

To my youngest child, Sandra, my partner at the Herbal Centre, for her love of lavender, for the testing and tasting, the baking, the mixing and making of all the recipes in this book, and for the lavender designs she creates, and the manufacture of the lavender products, my gratitude always, and specially for creating the lavender quilt for Shaun in the last days of her life. Shaun's wish, almost her last words to us, was 'to go into lavender quilt production', which we now do for her, to honour her wish, and the exquisite white silk quilts with Sandra's lavender design go out into the world to comfort others as it did Shaun.

Lavandula dentata *'Elegans' in the foreground and the giant* Lavandula intermedia *'Margaret Roberts' against the pillars.*

To Phyllis Green, our lavender photographer, who steeped herself in lavender, who inhaled lavender and who was there in every moment of her sparse spare time, in amidst her tightly packed schedule, to record on film the unfolding beauty of all the varieties in all the seasons, my most grateful thanks for the exquisite photographs.

To Reneé Ferreira, my managing editor, thank you for the enormous task of actually putting together my prolific writings, and getting it into order, for always being so enthusiastic, so careful, so professional and so supportive, and who fetches and brings the neat manuscripts backwards and forwards over long distances to fit in with all my exhausting commitments. A book like this could never happen without you!

To Annatjie van Wyk who types my handwritten miles of pages, who deciphers the small-hours-of-the-morning-prolific outpourings and who keeps track of everything and who knows what I am doing in all my diversity, I am eternally grateful to you and to the farm postbox where I can deposit the bunches of pages in the cool dawns, knowing the contents will be spirited away to Reneé's desk – oh, the wonder of technology – before the day begins in earnest, neatly e-mailed and in order.

To my new publishers, Briza, my gratitude for the warm and enthusiastic freedom you give me to just write – no restrictions, no urgency, just support. This is the first book of several they have commissioned – I look forward to being one of Briza's authors in a bright future.

To the farmers and the commercial growers, to the dedicated growers and nurserymen, like Brian Krull of Plants' Management South Africa, both in South Africa and abroad, with whom I share the lavender passion, thank you all for urging me on to record our findings and for helping me to establish the lavender register in South Africa. Without you, each one, I would not have been able to set out the trials with such diversity. And as this book begins its journey, I need to record the backing of two of South Africa's most esteemed horticultural businesses. Firstly Ball Straathofs, the seedsmen, who deliver the richly varied Margaret Roberts Herb Seed Collection, including the lavenders and groplugs of the lavenders for the commercial growers, to all the corners of our great land. Secondly to Malanseuns, the biggest growers in the Southern Hemisphere, who will distribute countrywide the fascinating and unusual lavenders and all the new herbs, including the Margaret Roberts lavender, and – for the first time in the world – the new *Lavandula dentata* 'Margaret Roberts Elegans'. Botanical history is being made with these joint ventures – 'plant partners' the nursery world quips – and we are united in getting both seeds, plants and information to you wherever you are. What a future!

FOREGROUND: **Lavandula stoechas** '*Marshwood*'.
MIDDLE: **L. pterostoechas** '*Blue Canaries*'.
BACKGROUND: **L. stoechas** '*Avonview*' *now called* '*After Midnight*'.

I also need to thank the many students at our Herbal Centre classes who have tried and tested the lavenders in their many diversities, the young chefs and hotel school students for testing the lavender cuisine, and the beauty schools for testing the lavender cosmetics, their enthusiasm has spurred me on!

Here too I need to give my hugest thanks to Woolworths, to my mind South Africa's most superb chain of shops, and to thank them for allowing me to develop with them the 'Lavender experience' that has driven the shoppers wild. Thank you Woolworths for the superb lavender products we have together created, from bed linen to towels to pyjamas and gowns to stationery and special occasions gifts, and for the exquisite core range of Margaret Roberts lavender toiletries. I am proud to be a part of so magnificent a production line and to have been 'married' to Woolies for so many years. Woolworths has brought the lavender ranges to your doorstep, and into your home again and again to fulfil their mission of giving the customer what she wants. I am frequently stopped in the street by grateful Woolworths customers thanking me for giving them a lavender pillow to sleep on, a lavender duvet to sleep under and lavender soap and bath salts to bath with, and on, and on. Woolworths makes it happen, so everyone can experience the lavender collection!

Lavender has been around for thousands of years, but is relatively new in South Africa – only about 100 years old. I'd love to think the varieties we grow today and record in this book will be around for thousands of years. Let's start today and make a lavender garden and share our lavender passion with everyone in this great country and beyond.

The Herbal Centre
De Wildt
North West Province
South Africa
Summer 2003

Note to the 2006 impression
There have been a number of name changes recently, for example *Lavandula intermedia* 'Margaret Roberts' is now called *Lavandula* × *heterophylla*. For the latest classification refer to *The GENUS LAVANDULA* by Tim Upson and Susyn Andrews, published by Kew, ISBN 1 84246 010 2.

Lavandula intermedia *'Margaret Roberts' is a cross between* L. angustifolia *and* L. latifolia.

Introduction

Lavender in all its forms and varieties, is, without doubt, one of the world's favourite herbs and never more so than at present – it could be called the designer plant of the new century.

I am often asked what is my favourite herb, and I think, all things considered, lavender is probably my favourite for its beauty, its versatility, its soothing, quieting, calming properties, and for its exquisite and nostalgic fragrance and its landscaping impact.

For many people lavender has been a loved childhood plant, a familiar scent in the linen cupboard and a staple posy and potpourri ingredient. I think back into my early childhood when I made my first tussie-mussies – those fragrant fat heads of the richly coloured French lavender circled my favourite little pink rose buds, or violets, or white daisies – a satisfying activity that has never left me. I still make tussie-mussies, more complicated now with circles of the different lavenders, and often for brides, and I always think of my grandmother and can smell her handkerchiefs and our little cotton socks she set out to dry on washdays spread on the lavender bushes that edged the lawn, and how she taught me the age-old art of 'posy-making', or 'tussie-mussie making'.

More than any other herb, lavender has been the first herb I became familiar with. I remember the big grey and mauve bushes my grandmother grew in her Gordon's Bay terraced garden and the picking of those richly scented flowers which we dried by hanging them up under the rafters on the back verandah. Then, in front of the fire on a winter evening, with the South Easter howling around the beach house and the small waves being lashed into an audibly angry sea, we stripped the little flowers from the stalks to make lavender sachets. The scent engulfed us like the sound of the wind and the sea. Then we tied the stripped stalks into bundles and tossed them onto the fire where they crackled and popped and the scent of the burning lavender filled the room. A safe and happy childhood, with those simple activities that I drew strength from in the bad times when the picking and drying of lavender and the stripping and sewing of sachets quieted the pain and the loss and the fears.

I found seeds in the little sachets I made with my grandmother which after so many years still had the faint smell of lavender. Those little seeds, just a small handful, germinated and gave me the first lavender bushes which I grew in the first farm garden I created when I married at 22 years of age and went to live on an isolated and distant farm. My grandmother came to visit me, and saw her lavender growing in that farm garden, and made a lavender sachet of pale pink silk for my second baby from the first lavender bushes that I grew. She died soon after that, but her lavender still continues to thrive. Thirty years later I put out into the marketplace that same lavender which I called 'Grandmother's Lavender' and found, after much research, its origins came from Spain to Britain, and from Scotland where my grandmother was born, and she brought it to South Africa as a young teacher in Stellenbosch around 1900.

Grandmother's lavender is a rare branched lavender, *Lavandula latifolia*, and although she called it Spike lavender, it has now been established that this wonderfully oil-rich lavender is one of the best seed producing lavenders in the Southern Hemisphere today, and its extraordinary scent lasts longer than any other lavender in dried form. So my Grandmother's lavender has made its mark. Wouldn't she be proud?

How I longed to tell her 18 years after she made the sachet for my second baby, under heartbreaking circumstances I had to leave that distant farm and start all over again in another inhospitable, hot, dry area, again on a mountain slope. I again carved out a garden and, bereft of all my herbs and fragrant plants, I had to start from scratch. Four seeds in her pink silk sachet were all I had to start my lavender collection. Three germinated and from those three seedlings I gradually built up the Herbal Centre lavender collection, and it all began with *Lavandula latifolia*, Grandmother's lavender.

Lavandula intermedia 'Compacta', possibly closely related to L. intermedia 'Grosso', flowers once only in late summer and is an excellent cut flower.

Today visiting lavender growers from Australia, New Zealand, Holland, Denmark and England have taken Grandmother's lavender seeds back to their countries with much excitement, assuring me it smells just like 'Oil of Spike', and perhaps this was originally one of the lavenders used in spike oil production around 1865. What is even more fascinating is that the cross-pollination of this lavender, *Lavandula latifolia*, with the true English

Part of the lavender trials: three-year-old L. dentata *'Royal Crown' in the foreground and five-year-old* L. allardii *'African Pride' in the background.*

lavender, *Lavandula angustifolia*, has formed the spectacular *Lavandula intermedia* species of which the Margaret Roberts lavender (which I originally named the Herbal Centre Giant lavender and the nursery trade has named Margaret Roberts lavender) is a part!

I joined botanical societies and botanical gardens in several countries around 1970 to get seeds and cuttings. Many were disappointingly slow and erratic to germinate, but by taking tours to England's herb gardens I was able to get seeds and later cuttings to start the trials which form part of my lavender collection today. What has emerged from my 40 long years of growing lavender is that the Southern Hemisphere supports several very tough groups of lavender, but the colder, moisture rich, Northern Hemisphere lavenders, of which the greatest part are the wonderfully versatile *Lavandula angustifolias*, visibly struggle to keep alive away from their colder, richer and wetter natural habitat.

The trials at the Herbal Centre gardens have been ongoing for the past 20 years and the last decade has been seriously logged and observed, and I have the many lavender growers from throughout the world who have visited my trials to thank for their input, advice and practical growing tips, and most importantly for their verification of the names of the different lavenders.

So it is with much trial and error behind me, much serious research over the past 30 years, and present research that constantly surprises and verifies, and with a future of lavender enjoyment before me, that I feel confident to put pen to paper at this age and stage of my life. Within these pages I will share with you all my accumulated knowledge on the lavenders, and the recipes and planting tips and ideas I have gathered over my life, loving lavender as I do.

In 1997 I wrote the *Little Book of Lavender* in the Margaret Roberts Little Book of Herbs series. It was out of print within six months and despite the pleas and beggings, the publishers never reprinted it, as not even the popular *Little Book of Basil* could top it. They felt the Little Books weren't the big sellers they needed. So for all of those who have begged for the *Little Book of Lavender*, here it is in grown-up form with all my many years of information that I hope will make lavender growing a pure and fragrant pleasure for each one.

I planted my 'field of dreams', it made good money, kept me sane, made me love life again, and gave back over and over every little hour of work I put into it, shaken together, pressed down and overflowing. A small piece of barren land that I dug and raked and planted and weeded and watered, and watered, often in desperation and with tears. Like life, it showed me how to withstand the droughts, the storms, the searing heat and the black and numbing frosts, and, like all things that you overcome, it gave hope and blessings and challenges and rewards of bunches of fragrance that put food on the table and shoes on my children's feet and in these latter years in a smaller new field of dreams, gave back so much interest and comfort when all else was lost, that without it, I too, would have been so lost I could never have found myself again.

I urge you to plant up *your* field of dreams – choose the spot and grab the spade. Work on a bite-sized piece each day – slowly, slowly it will happen. You alone can make it happen, and it's worth every moment.

In the language of flowers lavender means 'devotion'. I know what it means to be devoted to my lavender rows and the pleasure they give me cannot be measured. I wish each page of this book could be scented with lavender to take you into the magic of growing lavender, and then using it, living with it, and enveloping your whole life in it. It is such a worthwhile journey.

Growing lavender

Oil from lavender has been extracted in various ways for over 600 years. There are traces of lavender oil – still fragrant – in clay vials in several museums across Europe and Britain. It is still used medicinally today, as it was by monks in those early days of our history.

The name 'lavender' comes originally from the Latin word 'lavare' which means 'to wash', and it is one of those esteemed ancient herbs that was first used, perhaps due to its refreshing scent, to cleanse clothes, furnishings and baths, but the origins are lost in the mists of time thousands of years ago.

One of the earliest recordings was made by the Greek writer, Dioscorides, who compiled an authoritative list of the earliest medicinal plants – he wrote it in the first century AD – and one of the first lavenders ever to be recorded is *Lavandula stoechas*, commonly known today as Spanish lavender.

Think back to your grandmother's garden. There were usually one or two lavender bushes, mostly the favourite green *dentata* with its light blush of small flowers mainly in spring. And then, quite commonly, there was that big sprawling non-flowering grey hedge lavender that withstood neglect admirably. No one took much notice of it. It was known then as Lavender Spica.

Because my grandmother grew lavender for the flowers, I always thought that it was the done thing, and accepted her lavender as part of life. Later, when I married and went to live on a farm I found that my mother-in-law also grew a few bushes of lavender. Thirty years ago when a friend returning from France asked me to find 500 lavender plants for him to line his paths, the search was on. He ended up with rows of *dentata* lavender, always known as French lavender to this day. He was the first person I knew to plant lavender *en masse* and I was enchanted. I began cultivating in earnest, and that is what this book is all about.

LEFT: **Lavandula dentata** *'Royal Crown'.*

Soil requirements

Let us start by looking at the soil. The two basic requirements for the soil are that it be well drained and positioned in full sunlight. I have found that the best soil is light and sandy, ideally with a pH factor between 6.0 and 8.0. My best lavender grows in lightly composted soil with a pH around 7.0. But what is very encouraging is that most lavenders available today can adapt even if the soil is slightly acid. So I urge growers to give it a try wherever they are, by adding a little agricultural lime to increase the pH if at all necessary. When growers get technical and soil samples are sent backwards and forwards, I always suggest that they try a row of all varieties as an experiment and keep good records. This will help enormously for future plantings.

Climatic requirements

We have established that the Northern Hemisphere *angustifolias* have a difficult time adapting to our hotter drier Southern Hemisphere. We also know that the best oils come from lavenders grown between the latitudes 44° and 45° North with winters between 2 °C and 4 °C and summers no hotter that 25 °C, and up to 900 m above sea level, not to mention the regular soft soaking rain.

But, there is hope. The *intermedias* do well in hotter and drier locations especially in the Southern Hemisphere and don't seem to mind the sea levels. Again, it is just experimentation and

Top: Lavandula stoechas *'Kew Red' – six months old.*
Middle: L. dentata *'Elegans' – six months old.*
Bottom: Lavender trials showing three-month-old plants.

observation and try all the cultivars before you go into large-scale production. Most lavenders withstand cold well, but in heavy frost areas you will need to protect the young plants in their first one or two winters.

WATERING

The experts overseas say lavender does not like overhead sprinklers, but I have no option. My mountainside soil is so sandy and rich in fine gravel, that I cannot water in any other way, and my lavenders surprisingly thrive with overhead sprays. It is also good to remember that lavender is described as a drought-resistant plant. Its spring growth is enhanced by spring rain and careful water management thereafter.

The hottest and driest summers have taken their toll, so I always advise growers to have a reliable watering system in place as a back-up when rain is scarce. As water is so precious, and we all need to be aware of our dwindling resources, I have established that lavender does well with just a twice-weekly watering. Remember never to over-water as this encourages diseases and have drip irrigation to the roots if possible.

Six- to seven-month-old plantings of Lavandula intermedia *'Margaret Roberts' thriving at the foot of the great Magaliesberg mountain range.*

Avoid overhead sprinklers if at all possible, as they can cause the bush to sag and slit open, but as I mentioned before, I have no option but to make use of this method of irrigation. I manage this well, and all my lavender plantings, even the trials, have overhead sprinklers.

Lavandula dentata 'Royal Crown' is one of the best cut flower lavenders for small posies. It is a prolific flowering lavender. This bush is six years old.

WIND SHELTER

Ideally lavender should be surrounded by hedges or hills to shelter it from hot dry winds, as significant amounts of essential oils can be dispersed by buffeting winds. It's good to remember that the oils in the leaves and the flowers become more volatile as the temperature increases to over 28 °C, so shelter from wind is essential if the crop is being grown for oil.

I have planted elder trees 2 m apart as windbreaks. The elder flowers and berries are a useful crop for champagne, syrups and jams. (Be sure that you choose the correct non-suckering elder to plant.) The elders form a multi-stemmed 5 m high hedge and are good companions to the lavenders. A farmer in the cooler part of the country grows windbreaks of apple trees, and another grows almonds. In the hot areas pomegranates and quinces do well.

My summer temperatures often go up to 36 °C and 37 °C, and the *angustifolias* really struggle in the heat. They do better with the afternoon shade, but even so they still struggle away from the cool moist meadows of Europe.

Mulching definitely helps to conserve water and the drying effects of hot winds. The best is a mixture of grass and leaves packed in between the young plants, covering the surface to keep the soil cool.

PRUNING LAVENDER

Lavender is generally pretty tough, but pruning that is too severe will definitely stunt its growth. Often the bush will never recover. The flowers that are left behind after picking will need to be cut off, so hedge shears are easiest and in that way you can *lightly* tidy up and prune the bush. Never cut back more than ⅓ at the very outside of the bush. I usually find it does best with only ¼ cut away or even less. Don't be heavy handed.

Both the big old-fashioned Hedge lavender, *Lavandula spica*, now known as *L. allardii* 'African Pride', which usually grows to about 1.5 m in height and width, and the more compact large-leafed *Lavandula allardii* (Dutch lavender) can be more severely cut and even shaped. These two have very few flowers and sometimes never flower at all, so keeping them trimmed and neat is a pleasure, as all the fragrant clippings can be swept up and made into furniture rubs, bath scrubs and wonderful potpourris.

BACKGROUND: Lavandula intermedia *'Margaret Roberts'.*
In the foreground is Plectranthus neochilus, *which is a superb, easy to grow companion to lavender, and has similar beautifully shaped purple flowers. This plectranthus is also known as 'Spur flower'.*

For the *intermedias* like 'Grosso', all you need to do is clip off all the flowering stems and leave the bush in its natural neat rounded cushion. The big Margaret Roberts *L. intermedia* needs all the flowers trimmed and the bush slightly shaped. This needs to be done three or four times a year, as this is a perpetual all-year-round flowering lavender.

The *dentatas* need the old flowers clipped off and a little rounding and neatening every now and then. All the stems need to be cut back as lavender flowers on new sprigs. If you leave the old branches to do their thing you'll have shorter stems and smaller flowers.

Prolific all-year-round flowering of Lavandula intermedia *'Margaret Roberts'. These plants are used for cut flowers.*

After I have pruned I add a good bucket of compost and let the hose gently and slowly soak into the roots for a good length of time. This watering and composting lessens the shock and the plants recover quickly.

With perpetual flowering lavenders like *L. intermedia* 'Margaret Roberts' and the *dentata* group 'Royal Crown', 'Elegans' and 'Candicans' this pruning programme can be carried out three or sometimes even four times a year. With the *stoechas* group I do it after the spring flowering, usually in early November. In this way you can keep your lavender bushes for 4–5 years or even more. If you're using the flowers as cut flowers all the time I find replacing every 3–4 years works best, as I pick long stems, and as the bush ages the stems get shorter, and the florists want stems as long as possible. Interestingly, I have some lavenders that are over 10 years old that still produce flowers, and although the bushes are often a bit lopsided, they're still healthy and flowering.

FERTILISERS

I am a fanatical organic grower; I use only compost, but if we remember lavenders thrive on lime and compost, I suggest making up a concentrated booster by mixing a little lime and compost before planting and each winter thereafter. Bonemeal is also excellent and can be dug in every spring. Lavenders will not tolerate strong manures, especially chicken manure, so avoid manures and rather

Lavandula dentata 'Royal Crown' is loved by button-hole florists as it does not wilt or hang its head.

go for well-rotted and matured compost, which can contain manure, but having matured will no longer burn the tender roots, and make your own compost – this is the most economical way.

My first commercial lavender-growing venture in 1976 was on heavy black clay soil. It was a nightmare to dig, wet or dry, and it took an exhausting month to get the first two rows in. So I virtually gave up and with a pick hacked out 30 cm shallow holes and filled them with compost and added earthworms wherever I could find them. I found to my amazement that there was no difference in size or yield. My next commercial growing enterprise, a decade later, was on sandy soil on a mountainside rich in quartz. I again dug a wide shallow hole the length of the spade, filled it with compost, lots of water and earthworms, and I have a thriving crop. Need I say more about the wonders of home-made compost? And *all* the varieties of lavender thrive in it.

Remember, when you're tempted to use fertiliser, that you'll be using your lavenders for food, cosmetics, bath preparations and medicine. Chemical sprays and fertilisers are simply not an option. The beauty of lavender lies in its healing properties, oils and fragrance. *It has to be pure and organic.* If you are an essential oil producer it is worth having your fields organically certified and registered so that you can claim that appealingly important fact: 'organically grown' on your label.

FRONT: **Lavandula stoechas 'Papillon' is fragile and fairly short in height.**
MIDDLE: **L. dentata 'Royal Crown' reaches almost a metre.**
BACK: **L. intermedia 'Margaret Roberts' reaches over 1½ metres.**

PROPAGATION

There are two methods of propagating lavender – one is seed, the other is cuttings. Lavender seed is notoriously erratic in germination, but it is still worth trying. In one packet of seed you may get several colour variations which are fascinating in their diversity, and you may even get a completely new colour that has not been seen before. I got the palest of mauves – virtually white – in a packet of lavender seed from England, and it is still true to form.

The rare and almost impossible to propagate Lavandula stoechas *'Viridis', a richly fragrant yellow lavender. Behind it is a sturdy* L. dentata *'Elegans'. Both are five-year-old bushes.*

SOWING LAVENDER SEED

I have been successfully collecting and sowing lavender seed for 30 years, and have had marvellous results from a few varieties. Not all lavenders produce seed, remember in general the *intermedias* are sterile. But we have been happily surprised through the years with *L. dentata* 'Royal Crown', *L. dentata* 'Giant Candicans', *L. dentata* 'Margaret Roberts Elegans', and my wonderful old favourite, my Grandmother's lavender an old English Spike lavender. The seeds of all of these come up like hairs on a dog's back.

Sow the seeds in sand-filled seed trays to which a small amount of light compost has been added. Seed trays need to be no less than 10 cm in depth and the proportion of compost to sand is 1 in 12. Mix well and keep moist. Sprinkle the tiny black seeds over the surface, which needs to be lightly pressed down. Cover with a dressing of fine sieved sand, enough to cover the seeds, and stand the seed box in a tray of water so that you water from the bottom. When you see that it is well soaked, remove from the water-filled tray and cover with a sheet of glass. Keep shaded and moist until the seeds germinate. Remove the glass once they are about 2 cm high. Never let them dry out. Thereafter keep watering daily, but give the little plants lighter shade.

When the little plants are big enough to handle, gently prick them out and transplant into compost and good soil-filled garden bags 15 cm in diameter. Keep moist and once they are established well, start bringing the pots into the sun gradually. Half an hour a day is long enough to begin with, then increase the time to an hour, and so on, over a period of two weeks. Always keep the plants moist, and in a month they can go out into the sun full time. When the little plants are tough and sturdy and about 12-15 cm high, it's time to plant them out.

Plant out into well-dug well-composted beds in full sun, usually about 1 m apart, in moist soil and water well. Water three times a week until they show a spurt of growth, thereafter twice a week and usually once a week in winter. If the area is very cold, cover the new bushes over the winter with little tents of coarse veld grass to protect them and mulch well with grass and leaves.

MAKING LAVENDER CUTTINGS

Select the best bush and take small thumb-length cuttings by pulling off non-flowering sprigs briskly from the branch. Leave the little heel that comes attached. Do not clip the sprigs off, pull them off with a sharp downward movement, grasping the sprig between thumb and forefinger, strip the lower leaves and press into a tray of wet sand about 10 cm deep. Make a small hole with a sharp stick, then press in the cutting to a depth of no more than 3 cm. Some growers dip the stems into rooting hormone to aid root formation before pressing the cutting into the wet sand. If you do this, use No. 2 for soft woodcuttings and wet the stem before dipping it into about 1 cm of powder. Press down well and keep moist. Press the cuttings in 2 cm apart.

Keep the tray moist at all times, and label and date the tray, and in cold weather keep it in a warm area covered with a large plastic bag over it to make a mini greenhouse. Press a few sticks into the corners to support the plastic – it should not touch the cuttings. Once the cuttings have formed strong roots – usually in about 6 weeks – gradually, and very gently, shake away the sand, and carefully, so as not to disturb the fragile root hairs, pull the cuttings apart and plant into bags filled half and half with a well-moistened mixture of compost and good garden soil.

Keep the bags shaded until the little plant has recovered, and in about 10 days start hardening it off by bringing it out into the sun for an hour each day and gradually increasing the time over a period of two weeks until the plant can stand a full day in the sun. Now it is ready to plant out in

well-dug well-composted soil in full sun 1 m apart. Keep well watered during planting time, thereafter three times a week. Once the plant is well established water twice a week and once a week in winter.

A showy splash of perennial colour lining a path. **Lavandula dentata 'Candicans' on the left and L. stoechas 'Marshwood' on the right.**

LAVENDER IN POTS

We are often asked whether lavender will do well in pots. The answer is that it will not do as well as it would if planted out in the garden. If you do plant your lavender in a pot use as big a pot as you can manage. Fill the pot with a layer of stones and a deep layer of well-rotted compost. Mix the compost half and half with sand. The sand is for draining and the compost for nourishing. For the top layer mix ⅓ good garden topsoil, ⅓ compost and ⅓ sand.

Stand the pot in a tray of water and let it get really moist, then plant the lavender deep into the moist soil. Lavenders grow big – no more than one plant per pot is advisable. Water from above to settle the plant then as pot plants dry out quickly, ensure that the pot never dries out by watering from below – stand the pot in a tray of water. Wilted lavender struggles to survive. Set a small drip spraying system into the pot so that it can automatically water two, three or even four times a day in hot dry weather once it is well established. This way you'll keep your lavender going for a long time.

Feed with a good organic natural fertiliser every month to keep your plant healthy. More than lavenders planted in the garden, potted lavenders need to be groomed frequently. All dead heads should be removed regularly. Remember, however, that even in large containers the lavender will need to be planted out in its second year. It will literally outgrow the container no matter how well-fed and well-watered.

I have found that the best varieties to grow in containers are *Lavandula dentata* 'Candicans', *L. dentata* 'Royal Crown' and *L. allardii* (Dutch lavender). *L. allardii* can be clipped into a neat shape.

HARVESTING AND PREPARING LAVENDER FOR MARKETING

As you gather experience in your lavender growing, you will become better at judging when to pick for cut flowers, dried flowers and oil production.

ESSENTIAL OILS

The more mature the flower the stronger it will smell and the higher the oil content will be. I have done many experiments through the years and have decided that my most successful pickings are when the flower head has the most colour.

It is the flowers that have the most oil, and although the fragrance differs in each separate plant, there are many things that we can be certain of. Virtually all lavender oils have varying amounts of camphor, linalool, terpenin, lavandulol, cineole and even linalyl acetate and borneol within the oils and extracts. These oils often have antibacterial, antifungal and antiseptic properties, and within these properties site and climate will also have an impact. So again I stress experiment and trial, and long before you decide to go fully into lavender cultivation set out rows and keep notes on your trials.

Oil production needs fresh pickings and some growers have mobile oil extraction units actually accessible near the field. My own fields were too small for automatic harvesters, so I used a small labour force with hedge-trimming shears. As a result my oils also contained a certain amount of leaves and stems.

CUT FLOWERS

For cut flowers I have found manageable baskets still the best method as the flowers wilt quickly. I would rather pick a few flowers and tie them into rough bunches and bundles, then quickly get them into water before starting out on the next basket load. Once the flowers have had a good drink you can take your time tying them into bunches. Never allow the flowering heads to go under water; they never fully recover from it.

A fabulous posy of Lavandula dentata *'Elegans'.* L. dentata *'Candicans' and* L. dentata *'Royal Crown' circled by* L. intermedia *'Margaret Roberts'. The yellow flowers are Toadflax, a perennial* Linaria.

A *tussie-mussie of* **Lavandula dentata** *circled by* **L. dentata** '*Elegans*'

As a rough guide it is usually a bunch of 100 stems tied with an elastic band, and then a bow of thin florist ribbon in mauve or purple makes it marketable.

TUSSIE-MUSSIES OR POSIES

Infinitely more exciting than cut flowers is the tussie-mussie or posy. I have made my best income with these, but it does take time. Place 100 heads of *L. dentata* var. *candicans*, *L. dentata* 'Elegans' or *L.dentata* 'Royal Crown' in the centre. These are the very showy French lavenders.

Tie well with two rubber bands, this is essential for the tussie-mussie to maintain its shape. Then circle with about 100 of the longer *L. intermedia* 'Margaret Roberts', spaced evenly around the French lavender. Again secure with rubber bands and then tie with mauve ribbon. Keep the stems only in water.

The spring-flowering *stoechas* lavenders can also be made into stunning tussie-mussies. My most beautiful was for a bride, starting in the centre with the short fat pinky mauve heads of 'Kew Red', circled with 'Devonshire Dumpling'– a deep purple – then circled with 'Pippa White' – a creamy white lavender– then circled with 'After Midnight' – once known as 'Avonview' – and a final circle of 'Pukehou' and 'Pippa White'.

All the shades of purple and pinky mauve with the creamy white 'Pippa White', which also edged the posy, gave it a bridal feel, and we used long mauve and white ribbons to tie it. Close your eyes and picture this. Bridesmaids dressed in lavender mauve, carrying posies of 'Royal Crown', circled with the *L. intermedia* 'Margaret Roberts', which also graced every table, with mauve tablecloths and candles scented with lavender. It was absolutely stunning and quite unforgettable.

DRIED FLOWERS

Dried lavender is easy. Use hedge trimmers to cut the flowers off as close to the foliage as possible. Dry the lavender on big plastic sheets in the shade. Turn them every day or every second day to aerate. It will take about

+–5 days for the flowers to dry in hot weather. Then literally thrash the stems to strip the flowers or work the bundles with gloved hands – the little lavender calyxes fall off easily. Work over the big thick plastic sheets.

Gather all the flowers together and sieve through a fairly coarse mesh to remove the bits, stems, odd twigs and branches. Store in dust-proof drums. The best lavenders to use here are *L. intermedia* 'Margaret Roberts' or 'Grosso'. The *dentata* lavenders and the *stoechas* lavenders can be tied in small bunches and hung up to dry. The flowers remain whole and dry prettily.

A posie or tussie-mussie made with white Tulbaghia fragrans *'Winter Bride', mauve* Tulbaghia fragrans *edging it and right round the outside* Lavandula intermedia *'Margaret Roberts'.*

The different types of lavender: classification of the Lavandula species

Often visitors to the Herbal Centre lavender gardens and the trial beds are amazed that there are so many different types of lavender. And it seems that the varieties and subspecies will continue, as lavender belongs to the great Labiatae family, renowned for easy cross-pollination like the basils, mints and rosemarys. How exciting to know that within your lifetime new varieties will have formed, stabilised, been named and established.

At present the genus *Lavandula* consists of well over 30 species of strongly aromatic small shrubs that are mostly native to the Mediterranean area. There are however a few groups of different types of lavender that grow in India, North Africa and even Arabia. What has caused confusion in the past is that every grower has a different name for the lavender that they grow best. This has led to complete chaos as far as identification is concerned. There is also often a natural hybridisation – so typical of the Labiatae families – giving rise to new hybrids whose parents we can only guess at.

Over the past decade or so I have worked with growers from England, France, Australia, New Zealand, Holland and Denmark on a general description of easily identified species. This will help us to identify the various groups that grow easily in our own country.

We have all agreed upon this and now all name our lavenders accordingly. You will still however find confusion out there, but if you know and understand a certain group of lavenders it does make things easier.

LEFT: The annual chamomile is a superb companion to all lavenders and seeks the protection here of Lavandula dentata *'Elegans'.*

LAVANDULA ANGUSTIFOLIA — ENGLISH LAVENDER

L. angustifolia is commonly known as English lavender. This is the Northern-Hemisphere lavender that is grown in those glorious fields of purple in Norfolk and Provence. It is *this* lavender that has that marvellous true lavender scent that all the world looks for. This is the lavender on which the oil industry has based its criteria. Once you have smelt this exquisite oil you will know its unique fragrance, and although other lavenders have a glorious fragrance *this* is the variety that is recognised throughout the world. What we must not forget is that most of the other lavenders have equally wonderful oils that *also* possess all the medicinal qualities that *L. angustifolia* contains.

Lavandula angustifolia *'Vera'* – *a difficult lavender to grow in our hot dry climate.*

The stunning pictures of the lavender fields in Norfolk and Provence make everyone gasp and this is what many growers want to achieve, but remember its origins and realise that *L. angustifolia* comes from a region situated 500–600 m above sea level. This is essentially a Northern Hemisphere lavender and needs cold winters, rain, cool climate, kind winds and preferably sea breeze.

The *angustifolias* have the widest size range of the lavenders. Some never reach a height of 15 cm, and they grow from compact to rangy and spread, rarely exceeding 70 cm in height. They have a breathtaking array of colours from white to pink, mauvy pink to violet, pretty pale lilacs, magentas and deep royal purples. This lavender only flowers once a year in summer.

DESCRIPTION

In all the *angustifolias* the leaves are linear shaped – this means smooth edges on elongated and revolute margins. The name *angustifolia* means narrow leafed. Usually these particular lavenders are grey leafed and the leaves are generally prolific. The colour-rich flowering spikes are either compacted in tight whorls or interrupted, with a basal whorl or two separated from the spike.

PROPAGATION

The flowers are fertile, so you can grow these lavenders from seed.

Intensely fragrant Lavandula angustifolia *'Hidcote' that survives, only just, under the heat of the African sun for about two years.*

ORIGINS

L. angustifolia is native to Europe – predominantly France, Italy, Spain and Switzerland – where it thrives in the cool moist meadows. By the seventeenth century France had established huge fields of lavender on the Côte d'Azur and Provence for the perfume trade. Growing lavender for this industry is still a viable concern.

Seeds were taken to England several centuries ago, where flourishing lavender farms and industries like Mitchum's Lavender and Yardley's Lavender were established. During Tudor times it was particularly popular for masking smells and warding off the plague.

OUR OWN TRIALS

My own trials have included *L. angustifolia* 'Vera', 'Munstead', 'Loddon Blue', 'Twickle Purple', 'Lavender Lady', 'Hidcote', 'Alba', 'Fring', 'Folgate', 'Maillette', 'Nana' and 'Swampy'. I manage to keep them going for one or two seasons only. They don't thrive, but I am still persisting with 'Maillette', the new 'Bee' and 'Swampy', as they show resilience to heat and drought.

Tiny, fragile delicate little Lavandula angustifolia *'Vera' was the first of the* angustifolias *to be trialled in our gardens. It hardly survived a season.*

L. angustifolia *'Hidcote' seems to be one of the stronger* angustifolias *but reaches nowhere near the size it does in England, its homeland.*

Lavandula angustifolia *Maillette*.

Lavandula angustifolia *Bee*.

The trials are ongoing – and viewable to growers – and, as this twenty-first century progresses I still hope there will be an *angustifolia* that adapts and flourishes in the Southern Hemisphere. I'll keep trying.

What is fascinating, and enviable, is that in New Zealand certain areas of alluvial soil have proved suitable for growing the *angustifolias*, and with its cooler temperatures – compared to France's south-eastern plateau, which is between latitudes 44° and 45° north, with cold winters of −2° to 4°, and summers around only 20°C, and the higher altitudes of up to 900 m above sea level – New Zealand does compare quite favourably. So perhaps somewhere in South Africa a similar habitat could still be found!

Lavandula angustifolia *Swampy*.

This is a typical flower of the intermedia group – *long stemmed, low-branching and tightly packed whorls.*

LAVANDULA INTERMEDIA

This is one of the most exciting cultivars of lavender to grow. *Intermedia* is a sterile hybrid between *L. angustifolia* and *L. latifolia* and the plants are usually bigger and more robust than the *angustifolias*, and it grows well here in South Africa.

They make magnificent cut flowers, and were once known as the Lavandins because of their powerful scent, which increases as the flower matures. This strong fragrance makes them ideal for crafts, fresh and dried flowers and oil production. They are used overseas in the nursery trade as a garden ornamental and a low hedging plant. I have had tremendous success with 'Grosso'; its high yield of essential oil makes it a popular choice with growers.

I have had tremendous success with one of South Africa's own *intermedias*, the 'Margaret Roberts' lavender, which has been so named by the nursery trade.* There are no plant breeder's rights or royalties on the *L. intermedia* 'Margaret Roberts'. Its name came about because it cross-pollinated in the Herbal Centre gardens around 1990 from *L. latifolia* (Grandmother's lavender) – the only *latifolia* we grow – and one of the *angustifolia* trials.

* Now named *Lavandula* × *heterophylla*

38

Lavandula intermedia *'Margaret Roberts' with yellow* Rudbekia *in front.*

A huge vigorous bush has emerged that grows 1.5 m high and wide. It is a perpetual flowering lavender with masses of flower whorls along the stems and the occasional branching stem off the main stem. Showy and prolific, this is excellent for cut flowers. It is also the best to grow for dried flowers as it dries beautifully and retains its fragrance.

I find that because I cut so frequently – I use shears – I need to replace the bushes every 3–4 years to keep the length of stem the florists need. Overseas growers are bowled over by it, as they compare it to 'Grosso', which is a far more compact bush with beautiful flowers. But 'Grosso' flowers only once a year whereas

'Margaret Roberts' flowers throughout the year. Trials in Holland, New Zealand and Australia are positive and exciting. The joy of *intermedias* is their tough strength and adaptability. So for cut flowers, dried lavender and oil, this is the one! 'Grosso' is now being accepted worldwide as an excellent oil producer.

But, always remember, the oils are different in the various cultivars and these *intermedia* oils do not have the same constituents that the *angustifolias* have. *Intermedia* oils are high in camphorenes, borneol and linalyl acetate, all of which alters the fragrance, but not necessarily the medicinal and cosmetic value.

Unfortunately, Europe looks only at the *angustifolia* components, so exporting our lavender oils is difficult, often impossible, but our own market has enormous potential to absorb these oils. I, for one, much prefer the *intermedia* oils, and use them extensively in my creams and lotions.

DESCRIPTION

L. intermedia 'Grosso' is neat and compact, and forms a beautiful pale grey cushion about 70 cm in height, from which masses of pale mauve flowering spikes arise in midsummer.

Close-up of **Lavandula intermedia** *'Margaret Roberts', the largest of all the* **intermedias***. Space bushes 2 m apart.*

Lavandula intermedia 'Grosso' – note the occassional branching stem. It flowers once a year only in midsummer. The fragrance of 'Grosso' has definite angustifolia overtones – this is what makes it one of the best oil producers in South Africa.

PROPAGATION

All the *intermedias* can be propagated by taking cuttings of non-flowering sprigs, the length of the index finger. Strip off the lower leaves and press into deep planting trays of wet sand. See also page 26.

ORIGINS

L. intermedia 'Grosso' has been around a long time. It is sometimes known as 'Wilson's Giant' and 'Dilly-Dilly' in Australia and New Zealand. Named after Pierre Grosso, who also introduced the *L. angustifolia* 'Maillette', 'Grosso' has been found to be suitable for oil production. Of all the *intermedias*, it is perhaps closest to the *angustifolia* oils.

We have named this midsummer flowering intermedia lavender Lavandula intermedia *'Compacta', as it seems to be a close relative, all the experts feel, to* L. intermedia *'Grosso'.*

This hybrid was discovered by Pierre Grosso in France in 1972. It was resistant to the yellow mycoplasm decline that infected whole fields of *L. abrialii*, so it became an important crop.

Lavandula intermedia 'Compacta' was brought to South Africa in 1990 by a botanist from France who came to the Herbal Centre gardens to see the Margaret Roberts *intermedia*. We grew it from that single cutting and were very unimpressed as it looked very much like the unflowering 'Richard Grey' lavender which has *never* flowered, but we kept making cuttings from the neat grey bush.

Imagine our surprise four years later one midsummer morning to see its flowers emerging! Tall unbranching pale bluey stems closely growing together, very much the way

Lavandula intermedia '*Grosso*' *before its midsummer flowering. Note the neat shape of the bushes.*

'Grosso' flowers, with tiny, very pale blue flowers that lasted two months on the bush and the butterflies loved it!

The French botanist had called it 'large-leaf type *angustifolia*', so we called it 'Compacta' due to its tight cushion of grey leaves and awaited the right name from visiting overseas lavender growers. We're still unsure of its identification, as are they, so 'Compacta' has remained, but they identified it as an *intermedia*. After that spectatcular flowering in 1994 it hasn't done much again and for the last four years we've not had a lot of show off. One Australian grower thought it could well be *L. intermedia* 'Grappenhall' and that is the closest we can get.

It has the habit of dying back in portions, so we're not going to use it in long-term plantings, but its leaves smell wonderful and we're waiting patiently for another show of midsummer flowers!

PLANTING NOTES

Intermedias are reliable and attractive. Plant 1 m apart. They can take clipping and neatening where needed. Plant *L. intermedia* 'Margaret Roberts' 2 m apart.

VARIETIES

L. intermedia var. 'Abrialii'

'Abrialii', introduced from France where it was grown before 1935, is rounded, neat and reliable. It has done well in South Africa. This variety flowers only once a year – midsummer – producing beautiful bright mauve tall flowers. It is popular as an oil producer and a cut flower.

Lavandula intermedia varigata 'Silver Ghost' is a neatly rounded and compact bush which will look good as a low hedge, neat and uniform.

L. intermedia var. 'Sumian'

This is presently being trialled in our trial beds, and so far has withstood a cruel summer of devastating heat and drought. 'Sumian' comes from France where it is used more as a cut flower.

L. intermedia var. varigata

This variegated pale and interesting lavender has been in our 2002 trials which we were told was 'Silver Ghost'. The leaf margins are creamy white and its growth is charmingly rounded and compact. Our Australian visitors think it is 'Walberton's Silver Edge' and in early 2003 Malanseuns growers brought in a new *Lavandula intermedia*, *Lavandula* 'Goldburg' var. 'Burgoldeen' – known as the Golden lavender it has a yellow margin on the leaves like the white edges on 'Silver Ghost', which is almost the same. We've kept to the name 'Silver Ghost' as no flowers have yet appeared on any and we're trialling these unusual lavenders in anticipation.

'Silver Ghost' grows to about 40 cm in height and width and *L. intermedia* var. *varigata* is over 50 cm in height. All form neat round cushions and have at this point no flowers, but according to New Zealand growers the flowers are 'Grosso' type but sparse and flower in midsummer. We'll keep watching for 'Silver Ghosts'!

Several *intermedias* are presently finding their way into South Africa: 'Super', 'Jaubert', 'Impress Purple', 'Grappenhall' and 'Chaix', to name a few. It will be fascinating to see which ones become the favourites. I am finding this group of lavenders infinitely rewarding and reliable, and our trials continue.

Why waste time with the difficult lavenders like the *angustifolias* when there is this superbly weather-resistant group of lavenders to be experimented with? Interestingly, a French visitor to the Herbal Centre, on smelling and carefully inspecting a bunch of fragrant 'Grosso' said that it competed favourably with some *angustifolias*. She always sought out 'Grosso' at the Saturday markets on the outskirts of Paris, as she loved the stem lengths and the fragrance. What are we waiting for?

LAVANDULA STOECHAS – SPANISH LAVENDER

Known as the Spanish lavenders, these lavender cultivars are varied, exciting and different with a cluster of bright bunny ears topping a little four-sided cone. They are the hybrids that flourish, with more and more new varieties appearing every couple of years, as a result of cross-pollination. The name 'stoechas' is from the Greek name Stoechades Islands – now called 'Iles de Hyeres' – close to France in the Mediterranean area. This lavender originated from these islands and the Spanish Mediterranean region.

Lavandula stoechas *showing the typical four-sided cone of brilliant colour and the bunny ear top.*

DESCRIPTION

A multicoloured fascinating group of lavenders, all the *stoechas* lavenders have a cone-type of flower studded on four sides with tiny flowers in pinks, mauves, some almost black, greys and even greens. The beautifully brilliant bunny ears that top the cone are veined and bright and vary in colour and length. The Spanish call it 'crowned lavender' and the little bunny ears crowns are spectacular.

PROPAGATION

This group of lavenders is generally sterile. It propagates from cuttings easily and reliably with the odd 'sport' coming to the fore from parts of the flower, which are sterile. Set cuttings in wet sand, and keep moist until they root.

ORIGINS

It is fascinating to learn that this lavender – the Spanish lavender – has been cultivated since the Middle Ages. It has been used as a strewing herb on floors, under bedding and behind tapestries since the earliest centuries. Ancient Greeks and Romans used this lavender in their laundries, bath houses and on the floors of their banqueting halls.

Another frequently used and much loved strewing herb was Micromeria or calamint, *Calaminta ascendens*. Archaeologists have found remains of both Spanish lavender and calamint in ancient bath houses and banqueting halls, and, incidentally, have even managed to germinate the seeds of the calamint, which we now grow!

Note the difference in size, shape and leaf growth. From left to right: Lavandula stoechas *'Purple', 'Sugar Plum', 'Devonshire Dumpling', 'Pippa White', 'Viridis', 'Helmsdale', 'Kew Red' and the tiniest of all, 'Snowball'.*

In the foreground is Lavandula stoechas *'Plum' and behind it* L. stoechas *'Pippa White' with white* Tulbaghia fragrans *'Winter Bride' in the background.*

Mass plantings of 'Avonview' (now called 'After Midnight') in spring are spectacular.

OUR OWN TRIALS

I am intrigued by the *stoechas* group. It is so variable and in spring and early summer is an absolute blaze of colour. Planted *en masse* it is breathtaking and gets visitors so excited. We sell out all our *stoechas* plants, no matter what variety, in that heady brief spring lavender festival we hold yearly.

To date we have trialled some 30 varieties of *L. stoechas* and have come up with our steadfast favourites. We chose these not necessarily for their flowers but also for their neat all-year-round appearance. The bushes can be clipped into neat hedges or tidied up, so it is possible to keep them looking good at all times with or without flowers.

Most of these cultivars are the result of cross-pollination and a few of them may even flower a short sparse burst in midsummer. If you are aware however that the *stoechas* group is mainly a spring flowering group you won't be disappointed.

PLANTING NOTES

Plant 1 m apart in well-composted well-drained soil in full sun. Dig in a little compost, about 4 spade loads, after the flowering period, and in midwinter. Some plants will reach 1 m. in height but usually they are around 80 cm in height and width.

VARIETIES

L. stoechas var. 'Avonview'

This is now known as 'After Midnight' due to confusion in registration.

It is one of the most reliable and showy varieties of the *stoechas* group, and normally reaches around 80 cm in height. 'Avonview' was discovered by a grower, Ross King, in New Zealand around 1990. It reached South Africa in 1994 and has flourished here ever since. We still have some of those original plants and we keep growing it.

L. stoechas var. 'Helmsdale'

Lower-growing 'Helmsdale' reaches 60–70 cm and has a dense greenish foliage with a deep velvety look, almost wine red. This very distinctive plant with definite dark red colour makes an interesting cut flower. I love it and have planted it as a walk edging with 'Papillon'. 'Helmsdale' was raised by Geof Genge in New Zealand around 1988 and only reached South Africa in 1994.

Lavandula stoechas *'Helmsdale' thrives in hot, dry conditions and makes a good low hedging plant landscapers find reliable. It remains robust and uniform and even without flowers makes a trimmable neat feature.*

Fragile and bright pink, little 'Papillon' is one of the smallest of the stoechas *lavenders.*

Lavandula stoechas var. 'Papillon'

This is a very different little *stoechas* lavender. It has small flowers with long brilliant cerise pink bunny ears and is somewhat loose and rangy. Although it is upright, it is beautifully showy and lasts a long time in posies and dried potpourris. This bright, dainty variety is also sometimes known as 'James Compton'.

L. stoechas var. 'Marshwood'

'Marshwood' reaches 1 m in height, and is another of Geof and Adair Genge's New Zealand lavenders. Like 'Helmsdale' it was named in 1988 and only got to South Africa in 1994. This variety has a definite palish mauvy pink look, with almost black corollas. In partial shade it goes a paler mauve. Magnificent in mass plantings and used as a cut flower, 'Marshwood' is a beautiful shrub. It needs a bit of pruning after the mass of spring flowers to keep it in shape.

Lavandula stoechas 'Marshwood' makes an excellent clipped hedge – the spring flowering is breathtaking.

L. stoechas var. 'Pippa White'

This has been a fascinating *stoechas* lavender to grow. It reaches a height of 70 cm and is the first of the white lavenders to come into the arena. Creamy white bunny ear bracts top a long flower with purple corollas, and the smaller 'Pippa Pink' has pale pink bracts. Beautiful as a cut flower, it does well with good pruning and looks good in the garden. We found at the end of our third season that the flower heads broadened and mutated, but after good pruning reverted back to normal.

'Pippa White' – the first of the white stoechas *lavenders to come into the country and it thrives, spectacularly!*

'Pippa White' was developed and raised by Peter Carter in New Zealand in 1992 and arrived in South Africa around 1998.

Lavandula stoechas var. 'Kew Red'

This was the first of the pink lavenders and grows to a neat small compact shape with masses of short fat rosy pink flowers in spring. Tiny delicate leaves are full of fragrance, and it fascinates everyone as it bravely sends out its mass of little unmistakably rose-red flowers. It has a more compact growth and reaches about 50–60 cm in height, it originates in Kew Gardens.

A truely pink lavender, Lavandula stoechas 'Kew Red' is at its showiest in late winter and spring.

L. stoechas var. 'Sugar Plum'

This is a definite browny lavender, cousin to 'Plum'. Both grow about 60 cm high and I use them as front-of-the-border plants. The bracts in 'Sugar Plum' are browny purple and the corollas deep purply-blue. This is another New Zealand lavender released in 1990. 'Plum' has a similar habit. I am fascinated with 'Sugar Plum', its colour is so unusual in a lavender. It's a collector's dream and flowers spectacularly, even on a tiny bush!

Lavandula stoechas *'Sugar Plum' close-up of the browny bracts – it's spectacular!*

Lavandula stoechas var. 'Devonshire Dumpling'

This is a lovely little bright purple stoechas lavender that forms a neat compact cushion and a mass of flowers in spring. It is a new lavender from England, and like 'Kew Red', has small fat compact flowers. It is a great favourite with gardeners as its growth is compact and about 50 cm in height.

Grow the reliable little Lavandula stoechas *'Devonshire Dumpling' as a path edging. It looks good all year round, even without flowers.*

L. stoechas var. 'Snowball'

This is the smallest of the *stoechas* group, and our trials over three seasons have found it to be reliable, neat and compact with tiny pure white flowers, which is so unusual. We snip off the flowers in late spring and the little bush remains rounded and neat. It reaches no more than 30 cm in height.

Lavandula stoechas 'Snowball' is a little ball of purest white. Rare and exciting, it's a show of snow in spring and a neat round bush all year through.

L. stoechas var. 'Viridis'

This is the rare and exquisitely fragrant yellow lavender. It grows up to 1 m in height and has atypical limy green leaves. This lavender comes from Spain, Portugal and Madeira, and it is thought that it was used to scent the washing water, particularly in Portugal in the Middle Ages. It was sewn into the hems of the bishop's robes to protect him from the plague, and was spread under the matresses of priests and church deacons.

Revered and respected, this was probably the lavender that was used in soaps, furniture and floor polishes and boiled with water and used as a rinse for linens and woollen clothes. Fascinatingly, it was grown as a commercial crop in Spain around 1800 and oil extraction was tried and abandoned, but it was still cut and used fresh as a strewing herb.

Rare and exquisite, Lavandula stoechas 'Viridis', a true yellow lavender, is headily fragrant, particularly the leaves, but almost impossible to propagate here. We think it's too hot for it.

This is the first of the Lavandula stoechas *plants to come to South Africa – named* L. stoechas *var.* stoechas. *From this many varieties of Spanish lavender have arisen.*

We have one sturdy bush in the lavender gardens. It has been there for nine years, and has been neglected. The monkeys – who love lavender and romp in the plantings – have broken it, jumped on it and flattened it many times, but it still survives. I am astonished and filled with respect! Cuttings from it do not seem to take, but we are persisting.

There are an enormous number of *stoechas* lavenders constantly being named and coming to the fore. In our trials are the old-fashioned original *stoechas*, simply known as *L. stoechas*, *L. stoechas* 'Winter Purple' does well with us, as does *L. stoechas* 'Butterfly Blue', 'Pukehou' and 'Pedunculata', which by the way was one of the first *stoechas* lavenders to be called Spanish lavender.

The Romans and Greeks were familiar with several varieties of *stoechas*, and the Spaniards took mattresses and pillows filled with *stoechas* lavender sprigs on their voyages across the oceans. One of those lavenders would probably have been *L. stoechas* 'Atlantica' as it grows abundantly in Spain and Morocco.

New varieties will continue to rear their pretty heads, and as the *stoechas* group does well all over the world, here's hoping that the new ones will come to the Southern Hemisphere as well.

Lavandula dentata or French lavender. In some ancient Herbals it is called 'toothed lavender'.

LAVANDULA DENTATA

This is the old-fashioned 'toothed' lavender – hence the name 'dentata' and it was one of the first lavenders grown in the Southern Hemisphere.

All are showy and continuously flowering pretty shrubs. They make spectacular borders and low hedges, are exquisite in posies or tussie-mussies, and last well as cut flowers. They can also be dried for potpourris.

The wonderful thing about *dentatas* is that they always look good. I can remember as a child the original little *dentata* withstanding heat, drought, winter winds and frosts, yet there were always enough flowers to pick to surround the silver candlesticks on the big polished dining-room table, and enough space on

— 57 —

the bushes for my grandmother to spread out her freshly washed handkerchiefs and our little white socks to dry. This was the scent of childhood. Her lavender (Grandmother's lavender) was planted alongside the *dentata* rows, so all our drawers and cupboards smelt of the rich fragrance of these lavenders. Green *dentata* can still be found in old gardens across the country today.

Now with the bigger and better *dentatas*, its spectacular flowering habit makes this group of lavenders a popular garden plant with everyone.

DESCRIPTION

These lavenders all have a fat little head of 'scales' and tiny flowers within the 'scales' topped by a small crown of purple bracts.

This is the original 'green dentata' *known as* Lavandula dentata dentata.

ORIGINS

This was one of the first lavenders grown in the Southern Hemisphere. It is thought to have originated in the Mediterranean area and along the coasts of France, Morocco, and as far across North Africa as Tunisia.

VARIETIES

The original *dentata* lavender or 'fringed' lavender as the English call it, is a small-flowered green *dentata* with fine leaves, which is now known as 'green *dentata*'. From this brave little mother plant several varieties have come, including the cross-pollination of *L. dentata* 'Candicans'. Let us take a look at the varieties *L. dentata* 'Candicans', *L. dentata* 'Royal Crown' and *L. dentata* 'Elegans'.

Lavandula dentata var. *candicans*

OUR OWN TRIALS

Candicans definitely varies in the category *L. dentata* var. *candicans*. My first *candicans* plants came from America in 1993. The American growers, who got the plants from France in 1990, called it French lavender var. *candicans*. The bushes had bigger grey leaves, but they sprawled quite untidily. I love the definite grey of the leaves and the bigger cone-shaped flowers with their distinctive ears. I plant them as a hedge and under standard Iceberg roses, where they look spectacular.

In 1995 a large-flowered *candicans* came to the Herbal Centre gardens with the Australian growers, who also named it French lavender, *L. dentata* var. *candicans*. The size of the flowers is spectacular, often the length of my thumb. So to differentiate between the two I called this *candicans* 'Maxima' in our plantings.

Close-up of Lavandula dentata *var.* candicans *'Candicans'. This is one of the original plants that came from America.*

In a mass planting Lavandula dentata *'Candicans' is breathtaking. Its decidedly grey leaves are the perfect foil for the bright and colourful flowers.*

In the past two years, growers from Australia and Holland have seen the two *candicans* and agree that there are several slightly different varieties all going under the name *L. dentata* var. *candicans*. So we all agree that there are more than two definite grey-leafed *dentatas*, that their growth differs as does their size, but that they are still called '*candicans*'. It is well worth growing them all to see what they do in your garden. I pick them all through the year.

PROPAGATION

Replace the bushes from cuttings every 3–4 years.

PLANTING NOTES

Plant 1.5 m apart. I add extra compost for these big lavenders and I soak the hole thoroughly before planting. This gives them a good start and they flower immediately and are never without flowers. So, make sure they are deeply watered twice weekly.

This is the large flowered Lavandula dentata *var.* candicans *I have called 'Maxima'. Note the large compact flowers, some thumb length.*

These plants need the odd bit of pruning to shape them. They need little attention other than a barrow or so of compost twice yearly and a good weekly or twice-weekly soaking and dead-heading occasionally.

Lavandula dentata var. 'Royal Crown'
OUR OWN TRIALS

This one got me really excited! 'Royal Crown' has been around a long time The French say that this was one of the lavenders that grew in Monet's garden. I first grew it in 1990 in long mass plantings. Over a decade later I still have some of the original bushes. They are woody and small flowered, but still full of colour even if they're out of shape.

Lavandula dentata _'Royal Crown' is showy and prolific, its bright flowers are an all-year-round feature._

The leaves of this _dentata_ are green like their little mother, the 'green _dentata_'. The flowers, although not as long as _candicans_, compete beautifully as they are held very upright and are more prolific than _candicans_. Its little open crown of mauve ears sets it apart from the other _dentatas_. The bush is also neat and uniform and reaches 1 m in height and should be planted 1½ m apart, which makes these plants ideal for hedges, lining walkways and spectacular plantings.

What is so utterly charming about 'Royal Crown' is its constant abundant and colourful flowering and its resistance to drought, winds and storms. It even survives hailstones the size of chickens' eggs and comes up smiling! This hardy variety endures heat and cold equally well. The more you pick the flowers the more appear, and they make the most charming spring posies, circled with pure white narcissus and maidenhair fern and our lush white fragrant _Tulbaghia fragrans alba_ 'Winter Bride'.

Some growers have chosen 'Royal Crown' as a commercial crop as the flowers last well in water, tied into tight posies.

PROPAGATION

Propagation is by cuttings rooted in wet sand. Sometimes seed can be shaken out of a dried head after a good summer's rain. Although the bushes can be still attractive after 5 years, in order to keep the flowers good replace every 3–4 years.

PLANTING NOTES

Plant 1,5 m apart. For hedges plant 1 m apart.

All it needs is a barrow of compost twice a year and a deep soaking once or twice a week. Give it the odd tidy up and deadheading and it will give you years of pleasure.

For the cut flower market, plant 1½ metres apart. 'Royal Crown' lasts very well in water as a cut flower and dries with good colour for potpourris.

Lavandula dentata var. 'Elegans'
OUR OWN TRIALS

Following our mass plantings of 'green *dentata*' for 20 years, with the 'Royal Crown' for about 10 years, four years ago a cross-pollination must have occurred in the Herbal Centre gardens. We think –

Lavandula dentata 'Margaret Roberts Elegans' is the possible cross between 'Royal Crown' and the original small 'green dentata' and is one of the most spectacular dentatas to emerge. I have named it 'Elegans'.

A close-up of 'Elegans' clearly shows its compact flower that lasts weeks in water and is the most brilliant of all the dentatas.

and the growers from Australia, New Zealand, Holland and England agree – that 'Royal Crown' cross-pollinated with 'green *dentata*'. Remember that both have the green dentate leaves. An exquisite dark purple *dentata* then emerged from the union of these two varieties.

The flower of this 'new' *dentata* is long, thin and elegant. The little ears on top are a brilliant dark vivid purple and the bush is a beautiful rounded shape that reaches 1 m in height. It is spectacular! I have trialled it for four years hardly able to breathe, and early in 2003 gave it to South Africa's biggest growers, Malanseuns, to propagate. It is already out in the marketplace, waiting to enchant gardeners all over the country.

I named this new variety 'Elegans' because of its elegant shape, long aristocratic flowers and dramatic impact on the landscape. The nurserymen have named it Margaret Roberts *L. dentata* var. 'Elegans'. Plant breeder's rights are pending. Imagine the great thrill of having watched a lavender grow on my little farm daily under my eyes, unfolding from a funny little plant into a spectacular beauty that will be loved by gardeners everywhere. After 4 years of trials it gets more beautiful every day. I am so proud to have this exquisite lavender now grown and distributed by Malanseuns and I wish every gardener much joy in the growing of 'Elegans'. My cup runneth over and I only wish Shaun could be here to see it now.

PROPAGATION

Propagation is by cuttings and, surprisingly, by seeds as well. We have replanted many seedlings collected from under the trial plantings and they have flowered true to form.

PLANTING NOTES

The plants reach 1 m in height, so plant them 1,5 m or even 2 m apart. Apart fom a light trim to the bushes after a flowering period and a barrow of compost twice yearly it is tough and resilient to weather and wind.

Lavandula allardii – Dutch lavender

This is the fascinating hedge lavender, or Dutch lavender, that was discovered as a seedling in France around 1890, and was assumed to be a hybrid between *Lavandula latifolia* and *Lavandula dentata*. If you look at the leaves, which are the biggest and most vigorous of all the lavenders, you will see why.

A favourite hedge lavender with landscapers, Lavadula alardii can be clipped, shaped and pruned easily and safely and always looks good.

I love Dutch lavender for its compact growth, 'clippability' – one of my favourite made-up words – and its tough resistance to wind, storms, hail, searing heat, bitter cold, drought and floods, and it happily goes from 37 °C to below freezing and never turns a hair – or should I say a 'leaf'!

It is spectacular planted as a hedge, and if left unclipped will every now and then produce a few tall compact 'English lavender style' spikes of grey-mauve flowers that smell richly of camphor tones. It is this high camphorene ingredient that makes this lavender such a boon in the kitchen. We gather arms full of the prolific branches and rub them vigorously on kitchen tabletops, windowsills and countertops to keep the flies out.

Hedge lavender planted near a garden seat creates a tranquil corner to sit and rest in the fragrance.

When you clip your lavender hedge save all the clippings for scenting bath water. Toss under the hot-water tap as you run the bath or tie into a pure cotton bag and use with soap as a scrub. At the end of a long day luxuriate in a lavender bath, and after a long relaxed soak you will certainly feel the benefit of those soothing oils.

The flowers appear at odd intervals all through the year on mature plants and hardly ever on the first- and second-year plants. They will then appear unexpectedly in a sudden burst and not again. So one could say that this is one of the blind lavenders to which the grower from Holland said *L. allardii* belonged, as you can't predict the flowers.

DESCRIPTION

The leaves are two definite shapes in *L. allardii* – some smooth linear margins typical of *L. latifolia* and some definite dentate margins, typical of *L. dentata*.

PROPAGATION

Cuttings taken at any time of the year root easily in wet sand, and the fastest way of getting the hedge evenly and reliably started is to plant out the rooted cuttings into compost-filled bags and let them mature first.

ORIGINS

It is interesting that the Dutch claim this lavender as their own; it was planted in Holland in the early 1900s as hedges. A grower brought me a single cutting from Holland around 1979 and it grew so easily that I cultivated several plants from that single cutting. (By the way, the grower, a Mr. Van den Heffer, also took back seeds in 1979 from my Grandmother's lavender. So perhaps Grandmother's lavender has become a Holland lavender by now. The grower was ecstatic about the scent.)

PLANTING NOTES

For a hedge you need to space Dutch lavender at least 1 m apart, better still give it 1,5 m as the bushes can then grow into each other. Always plant in full sun. Give it a deep twice weekly watering and a good 3 or 4 spadefulls of compost, to each bush, twice or three times a year, particularly if it is being cut as a hedge. This is the one lavender that can be cut square top and sides and look good all the time.

OUR OWN TRIALS

Recent trials in the Herbal Centre gardens have given us another *L. allardii*, the new 'Jurat Giant'. It has literally taken off and got us all excited, because at 20 cm in height and width it started perfectly formed great big flowering spikes 45 cm long!

As the end of summer is in sight, this tough and vigorous new 'Jurat Giant' has reached 55 cm in height. It is 10 months old and still sends up the odd flower. We are going to test it in all sorts of situations to see how it does through the seasons. So far we're thrilled. Its full title is *Lavandula allardii* 'Jurat Giant'. I am sure that it will become a favourite for landscapers.

This is the old-fashioned Spica lavender, now named Lavandula alardii *'African Pride'. It flowers sparsely and infrequently and is grown usually as a hedge.*

VARIETIES

Another well-known lavender falls into this *allardii* group. This one was, and still is to an extent, commonly known by the name *Lavandula spica*. It is that huge 1.5–1.75 m high hedge lavender that hardly ever flowers. When it does flower, the flowers are long dull dark grey spikes with a touch of mauve, and the bush is predominantly light grey in colour. This variety, which was previously only known as blind lavender, was first grown in South African gardens around 1945–1950.

The theory is that it was brought into South Africa from the Mediterranean area, most likely France or Italy, at the end of the Second World War. It is thought to have been packed into soldiers' bedding, clothing and supplies to keep out insects. (It too has a high camphorene smell, and would have been used to keep weevils out of food and bed bugs and fleas out of clothing.)

The Spica lavender that grows along the Mediterranean coast has been named 'Devantville lavender' and Australian growers say that it is one and the same. We can only guess at its journey. Maybe a soldier returning from the war planted it in his homeland. So our old Spica lavender is now known as *Lavandula allardii* 'African Pride', as it grows easily all over South Africa and has become our country's own personal lavender!

It is definitely worth having a bush or two in the garden. Like the other *allardiis*, this variety lasts for years. This is one of the advantages of growing the *allardii* group – they are the longest lasting of all the lavenders. I have one huge bush which is 11 years old and still going strong. It has been pruned, cut back and chopped down, and comes up again with vigour from the roots, over and over.

The leaves, sprigs and branches can be used in potpourris and in the bath. Danish growers say it is still used today as a strewing herb in stables and chicken brooder rooms. And it survives the snow!

The name 'Spica lavender' is now old fashioned (see box), but if you know it as that, add 'African Pride' behind it and know that it is an *allardii*. You will notice that although its leaves are not as large as the Dutch lavenders it also occasionally sports a toothed leaf. Get to know this small and rewarding group of powerfully scented lavenders, the *allardii* group. They are well worth growing.

WHAT'S IN A NAME?

The name *Lavandula spica*, it has been decided, is misleading. Much of the blame for the confusion in the naming of the lavenders, can be attributed to Linnaeus, the Swedish botanist, who in the eighteenth century, devised the first rational system for classifying plants. This system is still in use today.

It was Linnaeus who regarded *L. angustifolia* and *L. latifolia* not as two separate species, which they most definitely are, but as one large specie or variety within that specie, and named it *Lavandula spica*. Because Linnaeus was so authoritative in his classifications and because he was a most esteemed and respected botanist, it was only in the twentieth century that the botanists addressed the confusion and reviewed the classification. So *Lavandula spica* was then finally recognised as an ambiguous name and has been literally outlawed.

Some Lavandula angustifolias *have in the past been named* spica – *but look at the flowers and you'll soon see the difference!*

What several commercial lavender growers abroad have decided is that the word 'spica' needs to be phased out, but that when describing *Lavandula allardii* 'African Pride', 'ex-Spica' can be used in brackets behind it, for the time being. The growers have also agreed that although it was thought that most garden forms of the English lavenders were probably hybrids of *L. angustifolia* and *L. latifolia*, these are fertile and the cross-pollinated *Lavandula intermedias* are sterile.

It is also interesting to note that recent surveys in France rated *Lavandula intermedia* 'Grosso' as the favourite of the oil-producing lavenders. In the sixteenth and seventeenth centuries *L. spica* was regarded as one of the best lavenders for oil production.

So we do have to be responsible and careful, for the sake of future growers, how we name the lavenders and the oils.

Lavandula latifolia – Grandmother's lavender

This small group of lavenders was once called 'spike lavender', 'oil of spike' or the 'Lavandins'. When you *smell* this lavender you'll understand the difference between it, as a Lavandin, and the other groups. It is powerful!

Description

These lavenders have lateral branches on their flowering stems. Some have a long flowering spike, with up to four sets of branches coming off it. The bushes are round and quite compact and this cushion remains consistent and from which in midsummer the flowering spikes arise.

Propagation

Both seeds and cuttings are quick and easy to get going. Sow the seeds in trays and pick out when big enough to handle and plant in bags to establish.

Grandmother's lavender, Lavandula latifolia, *coming into its midsummer flowering.*

Origins

Interestingly, this is my grandmother's lavender. Its origins are predominantly Europe, namely France, Spain, Italy, and we now know, even Scotland. This lavender however grows happily at a lower altitude (below 600 m), unlike the *angustifolias*. In Europe *L. angustifolia* and *L. latifolia* have crossed, as the natural hybridisation occurs easily, just the way it did here in our South African gardens, and botanically these crosses are known as the *intermedias*. So we can now be sure that this pure *L. latifolia* is one of the parents of *L. intermedia* 'Margaret Roberts'. Isn't it fascinating to trace back the origins?

PLANTING

Once the little seedlings or cuttings have been well established in bags plant out 1½ m apart in good compost enriched holes and water well. All lavenders need full sun and this one particularly does well in extra hot conditions. It will thrive with a deep twice weekly watering. Interestingly, during the *very* hot *very* dry summers it manages to look good when all else is wilting and half dead.

VARIETIES

Grandmother's lavender is the only *Lavandula latifolia* we have come across in our four decades of lavender growing and the visiting growers from other countries verify this as a true *Lavandula latifolia*.

The oil from this lavender, known as 'oil of spike', is so powerful it is used in paints, varnishes and heavy-duty soaps, and our own small experiments in oil extraction are offering exciting results.

All lavenders have disinfectant properties, as well as antibacterial, antiviral, antiseptic and antifungal properties. I would love to see oil producers go down this road with *L. latifolia*. Ball-Straathofs, who produce the Margaret Roberts Herb Seed Collection, are including it in the seed range from our organically-grown seed harvesting, so it will be readily available. This is the *one* lavender that has virtually a 100% germination rate. (Remember my old seeds? Even 30 years on they'll germinate!)

Here is the clearly visible branching habit on the flowering stem of Lavandula latifolia, *Grandmother's lavender.*

A mass of colour in winter, Lavandula pterostoechas var. canariensis is a fascinating landscaper's favourite when little else flowers.

LAVANDULA PTEROSTOECHAS

This is a purely ornamental group of lavenders, but I am yet to discover why it is called a lavender. Planted *en masse* they make a spectacular show, and with careful pruning and removal of dead leaves can give years of pleasure. They have no scent or taste of lavender, but it is their colour and unusual flowers that are so appealing. I still don't know however why they are grouped into the lavenders.

DESCRIPTION

Botanically this is known as a subshrub. It has heavily-branched stems and pinnate leaves, or bipinnate leaves, and is commonly known as 'fern-leaf' lavender. In all the *pterostoechas* lavenders, even the

73

original quaint little *canariensis*, the leaves are bipinnate and fern-like. I still think the gentle words 'fern-leaf' lavender are more appealing than *pterostoechas*!

A showy hybrid, Lavandula pterostoechas *'Blue Canaries' has plant breeder's rights.*

PROPAGATION

Cuttings of the fern-leaf lavenders are very easy to take and root easily, but do remember that both 'Blue Canaries' and 'Sidonie' have plant breeder's rights on them (see box on page 79).

ORIGINS

The distribution of this lavender is wide. It has been found in such far-flung regions as the Canary Islands, Tenerife, the Mediterranean regions, North Africa, Egypt, Syria and Arabia. It was once known as Arabian lavender, and has always been rare, delicate and exquisitely fragile. Yet it flowers bravely through the winter, when it is at its fascinating best.

VARIETIES

Lavandula pterostoechas

OUR OWN TRIALS

My first growing of the fern-leaf lavenders with their multi-tipped flowering heads was in 1988. I was brought a fragile *Lavandula pterostoechas* var. *multifida* by a French grower, who said that it was a fashionable pot-plant lavender. The fern-shaped leaves were pale grey green, very silky and covered in masses of silvery hairs. I was enchanted!

The erect branched flowering heads support brilliant purple little tufts of flowers that elongate with age. No one had ever seen anything like it. In the same year a professor from an Australian university brought me *Lavandula pterostoechas* var. 'canariensis', that came from the Canary Islands where it grows prolifically. He told me that whereas my little fragile *multifida* reached 0,5 m in height, this would reach over 1 m, and have smaller leaves and masses more flowers. Well, the leaves are smooth light limy green and the flowers are light bluey mauve on purple bracts, and in spring and winter it is a blaze of butterfly-enticing colour but has never racched 1 m in height.

PLANTING NOTES

Plant out rooted cuttings into bags to

On the left are two buds of L. pterostoechas *var.* canariensis *and on the right matured flowers.*

establish them well before setting out in well-dug, well-composted soil in full sun. This lavender needs a deep twice weekly water, and even three times a week in hot weather. Give it a twice yearly generous composting – 2 buckets per plant – and trim consistently.

Lavandula pinnata

OUR OWN TRIALS

Then a similar fern-leafed lavender was brought into South Africa by plant developers and they named it *Lavandula pinnata*. It too blooms in winter and spring and was very similar to *Lavandula canariensis*. Before we knew it, within the next decade we would become familiar with *Lavandula pterostoechas*

'Sidonie' and *Lavandula pterostoechas* 'Blue Canaries'. Both are also spectacular as winter-flowering lavenders, and apart from a tidy-up after the vigorous flowering period, they will survive without any trouble for 4–5 years.

Interestingly, both of these *pterostoechas* varieties have been bred far from their native lands. 'Blue Canaries' has *L. canariensis* as a parent and will grow taller, over 1 m in height, with masses of flowers. Ruth Brookman of New Zealand raised it around 1995, so it is a relatively new lavender, like 'Sidonie', another new cultivar raised around 1992 in Australia by Sidonie Barton and Ian Cunliff. 'Sidonie' is greyer in colour and also has the vibrant mauvy blue that 'Blue Canaries' has, but 'Sidonie' has bigger flowers, and is more a *L. pinnata* type. So it is thought that 'Sidonie' has *L. pinnata* as a parent.

Visitors to my lavender gardens are enchanted by them, and the brave little parent *L. canariensis*, who first came into South Africa so long ago, still sends up its bright little spikes of brilliant purple. It still

This is the original of the fern leaf lavenders,
Lavandula pterostoechas *var.* **canariensis,** *in its full winter show-dress.*

has pride of place in my plantings. Every winter I linger on the paths that skirt the mass of purple flowers and marvel at that one small cutting that was placed in my hands so long ago. I will always be

Lavandula pterostoechas 'Sidionie' has bigger flowers and soft downy grey fern-like leaves.

grateful to the old retired professor from the far-away Australian university who gave me the cutting. He grew lavender and loved the little wild one, *L. pterostoechas* var. *canariensis*. I also thank the French grower who brought *L. pterostoechas* var. *multifida* into the heat of Africa to find a home for it in a climate so different from that of France.

I thank these growers who travelled so far to share the interest of growing these beautiful fern-leafed lavenders. I am so thrilled that they came from so far away to put those cuttings in my hands and most of all I am so grateful that those little fragile slips took hold and established in the heat and dryness of Africa, and they are still here! Aren't plants amazing?

Lavandula pterostoechas 'Blue Canaries' in its winter blaze of colour. Cut back the flowering spikes once they have faded and you'll be rewarded with more flowers right up to the midsummer heat.

Plant breeder's rights (PBRs)

These are protected plants that bear the PBR logo, and may under no circumstances whatsoever be propagated, or sold, without written permission of the lawful agent. Royalties are payable on any plant protected under PBRs. All protected PBR plants are delivered with a royalty label in the form of an orange price and/or a coloured card, which may not be removed under any circumstances. This is an indication that the plant was obtained legally from a lawful grower.

Trademarks (TM)

The name of the plant is registered with the Department of Trade and Industries and protected under trademark. This means that nobody other than the registered agent may use the plant name. Where you see the sign TM Pending, it means the trademark is pending and the same rules apply.

Where you see this mark ® it is an indication of a registered trademark. GA means a Gentleman's Agreement has been made between growers for the privilege of being allowed to grow a specific variety which the agent or founder launched in South Africa.

All the above legal implications need to be strictly adhered to by all growers and even gardeners. Already there are several lavenders registered under PBRs that have come in from other countries like, for example, New Zealand and England.

When in doubt, discuss any propagation you intend to do with a trademark lawyer before you even think about it. There have been some devastating legal battles in our country already and, sad to say, the bottom line is always *money*, even in the beautiful world of plants.

So respect these registrations and salute the original grower who recognised the potential! It's quite something to develop and recognise a brand new, never-known-before-plant and to have the spunk to go down the time-consuming legal road. So keep your eyes wide open for those serious little labels.

Using lavender

Remarkably versatile, and surprisingly delicious, lavender can be used in many ways. It comes as a bit of a shock when lavender lovers who thought lavender was only used in fragrance, and in cosmetics, taste the culinary versatility certain lavenders possess! The fresh clean taste it imparts enhances many dishes, so that once you have tried it you'll find yourself experimenting, and who knows what masterpieces you'll create!

As lavender has a strong taste use it only sparingly – a little goes a long way! And best of all, lavender will find an assured place in the cook's garden. I find the best lavenders in cooking are the English type of lavender, *L. intermedia* var. 'Margaret Roberts' and 'Grosso' which has a taste similar to the *angustifolias*, which are used in European cooking. I have used both *L. angustifolia* and *L. intermedia* 'Grosso' and find them delicious. The *stoechas* lavenders can also be used sparingly but this depends on personal taste, some may find them too camphor-like, so it's your choice. Avoid the *dentata* and the *pterostoechas* groups, as these are not really edible.

Remember in all the recipes only use fresh lavender.

Now comes the most exciting part, the using of the lavenders that are growing so beautifully in your garden. This is the rewarding part not only for the gardener, but for the commercial growers, and these are some of the recipes that helped me put shoes onto my children's feet, and keep the home fires burning – I've been making lavender products and cooking with lavender for so many years, it has become so much a part of me I can't even remember a time when I didn't use lavender!

LEFT, FROM FRONT TO BACK: **Lavandula stoechas** *'Marshwood'*, **L. pterostoechas** *'Canariensis'*, **L. stoechas** *'After Midnight'* **and** **L. allardii** *'African Pride'* – all in their Spring glory.

Cooking with lavender

Let's start this exciting section with 'cooking with lavender'. Many people are so startled when you tell them that lavender tastes delicious. They remain disbelieving until they have tried it. When I wrote my first little book on lavender, we asked the visitors to the Herbal Centre to taste our recipe trials, and all the kitchen staff so enjoyed the look of surprise that covered their faces when they tasted some of the examples!

What is fascinating is that the new young chefs – many of whom have been part of our Herbal Cooking Classes – are using lavender in restaurants and hotel dining rooms at present. So, for commercial herb suppliers, don't leave out the lavender – it's becoming the new cuisine flavour!

A Cape garden club requested a whole luncheon around these recipes on a gala occasion when they invited me to give a talk on the lavenders, and the chefs had all the ladies in a flutter at the exquisite meal they prepared using these recipes. I hear subsequently all the members of that enthusiastic garden club grow the lavenders now and meet monthly to share more lavender recipes, and the interest is growing!

STARTERS

I love these little lavender nibbles and often serve them with drinks, as a snack or as a start to a meal. Their fresh taste makes them the ideal start to a rich meal.

LAVENDER CROUTONS

SERVES 6
about 4 slices bread
sunflower oil
2 tablespoons lavender leaves and flowers, finely chopped
 (use L. intermedia *var. 'Margaret Roberts' here)*

Slice the bread in small, neat fingers. Heat a little sunflower oil in a pan and add the lavender leaves, flowers and bread fingers. Stir gently with a spatula until lightly browned. Drain on crumpled kitchen paper towels. Serve hot with dips.

AVOCADO AND LAVENDER DIP

SERVES 6-8
1 large or 2 small ripe avocados
lemon juice
salt and coarsely ground black pepper
1 tablespoon lavender leaves, finely chopped
 (use L. stoechas *Spanish lavender here.*
 I love 'Avonview' – its new name is 'After
 Midnight')
parsley, finely chopped

Mash the avocado with lemon juice, salt and pepper. Add the lavender leaves and mix well. Sprinkle with parsley. Serve with croutons or crisps.

FRONT: Avocado and lavender dip
BACK: Lavender and black olive and tomato tartlets

LAVENDER CHEESE SQUARES

SERVES 6

6 slices brown bread
butter
2 teaspoons lavender flowers (use L. intermedia
    var. 'Margaret Roberts' or L. intermedia var.
    'Grosso' here)
½-¾ cup mayonnaise
about 1½ cups mozzarella cheese
cayenne pepper

Toast slices of brown bread, and butter while still
hot. Mix the chopped lavender flowers into the
mayonnaise and spread on the toast. Grate the
mozzarella cheese, sprinkle on top of the lavender
mayonnaise and dust with cayenne pepper. Place
under grill, and grill lightly for 4 minutes, or until
the cheese melts and bubbles and starts to brown.
Cut into squares. Serve hot with sherry.

LAVENDER AND BLACK OLIVE AND TOMATO TARTLETS

MAKES 6-8 TARTLETS

These tiny mouth-watering tartlets can have all sorts of
fillings, but this is my favourite.

SHORT CRUST PASTRY

60 g wholewheat flour
60 g cake flour
½ teaspoon salt
60 g soft butter, cut into small pieces
3 teaspoons lavender flowers, stripped off their stems
    (use L. intermedia var. 'Margaret Roberts' or
    L. intermedia var. 'Grosso')
1 tablespoon lemon juice
1 egg yolk
about 1-1½ tablespoons water

Sift flour and salt into a large bowl and add the
bran that has been left in the sieve. Mix in the butter,
and rub with fingertips until the mixture resembles
breadcrumbs. Add the lavender flowers and mix
well. Add the mixed lemon juice, egg yolk and the
water. Make it into a ball and work until mixture
comes away smoothly from the sides of the
bowl. Wrap in cling film and refrigerate for 30
minutes. On a floured tabletop, divide pastry into
6 or 8 portions and roll out thinly. Cut pastry out
in shape of individual little flan cases, and press
pastry neatly into flan cases and trim edges with a
knife. Prick bases with a fork. Bake on a tray –
spacing each little flan case neatly away from
its neighbour – at 200 °C for 5-10 minutes,
depending on the size. Check to see if it is starting to
turn golden brown and if it feels crisp. Cool on a cake
cooler. Handle carefully.

FILLING

1 onion, finely chopped (about 1 cup)
½ cup finely chopped celery
1 tablespoon olive oil
3-4 tomatoes, peeled and chopped
sea salt and black pepper to taste
1 tablespoon brown sugar
1 cup black olives, stoned and chopped
¾ cup feta cheese, chopped
pinch of fresh lavender flowers (use L. intermedia var.
    'Margaret Roberts' or L. intermedia var. 'Grosso')

In a pan fry the onion and then the celery in the olive
oil. Add the tomatoes and cook for 6 minutes. Add the
sea salt, pepper, sugar and black olives. Cook for a
minute until everything is well blended, then spoon
into the little pastry cases. Top with crumbled feta
cheese and lavender flowers. Grill for 2 minutes or
until the cheese has melted. Serve hot.

LAVENDER ASPARAGUS

SERVES 4

4 lettuce leaves
1 large tin or 2 small tins asparagus spears or
asparagus salad cuts
1 tablespoon lavender flowers, stripped off their stalks
(use L. intermedia *var. 'Margaret Roberts' here)*
4 tablespoons mayonnaise
about 8 rocket leaves, finely torn
salt and freshly ground black pepper
1 green pepper, thinly shredded
a few lemon wedges

Place a lettuce leaf on each plate – choose a crisp hollow leaf to hold the asparagus. Place asparagus spears or pieces neatly into the leaf shape. Mix the lavender into the mayonnaise and spread about a tablespoon over the asparagus. Decorate with the rocket leaves and the green pepper slices. Sprinkle with salt and pepper, and add a squeeze of lemon juice. Keep chilled until ready to serve.

ROASTED VEGETABLES WITH LAVENDER

SERVES 6

olive oil
1 brinjal, thinly sliced
2 big red sweet peppers, cut into strips
2 green sweet peppers, cut into strips
2 red onions, peeled and cut into quarters
2 sweet potatoes, peeled and thinly sliced
6 courgettes, sliced lengthways into quarters
3 beetroots, peeled and thinly sliced
2 tablespoons lavender flowers, stripped off their
stems (use L. intermedia *var. 'Margaret Roberts' or*
'Grosso' here)
salt and black pepper
2 tablespoons crushed coriander seed
a few lemon wedges
a few wedges of mozzarella cheese (optional)

Place all the vegetables onto a baking tray smeared with olive oil. Dribble a little olive oil over the vegetables. Pack the vegetables up on their sides to get the most sides roasted. Sprinkle with lavender flowers, salt, black pepper and crushed coriander seed. Bake at 200 °C for 10-15 minutes. Check to see if vegetables are cooked and crisp, but not blackened. Serve on small plates with a squeeze of lemon juice and a wedge of mozzarella cheese if liked.

SOUPS

I am mad about soups and make them throughout the year, not only in the winter. My grandmother was a great soup maker, and she told me at an early age that to be a good housewife and mother you had to know how to make a good pot of soup from leftovers, like the chicken carcasses from Sunday lunch, and bits and pieces from the vegetable garden. I helped her from the age of about 8, and have made a good healthy soup ever since.

Soups are a good standby. I call them 'comfort coping foods'. I always have a pot ready for whoever visits. When I come home tired, late, discouraged and too bone-weary to cook, I quickly heat up a small saucepan of one of my nourishing soups.

COOK'S TIP

Always keep the basic ingredients for soup in your kitchen cupboard, fridge and culinary herb garden.
In the kitchen cupboard always have: pearl barley; lentils; split peas; Worcestershire sauce; chicken stock cubes and bouillon cubes (if you don't have a chicken in the deep freeze); sea salt; black pepper; cayenne pepper; dried haricot beans, chick peas or black-eyed peas
In the fridge always have: leeks; onions; potatoes; carrots; celery
In the culinary herb garden always have: thyme; origanum; basil (there is a new perennial sweet basil that can take the cold); chives; mint; spring onions; celery leaves; rosemary; and of course L. intermedia var. 'Margaret Roberts'; L. intermedia var. 'Grosso'.

PUMPKIN AND LAVENDER SOUP

SERVES 6-8

For a winter evening this soup takes some beating, and it is quick to make.

about 4 tablespoons good olive oil
4 large onions, finely chopped
2 cups chopped celery
6-8 cups peeled, diced pumpkin
2 tablespoons crushed coriander seed
1 tablespoon cumin seed
1 tablespoon caraway seed
1½ tablespoons lavender flowers, stripped off their stems (use L. intermedia var. 'Margaret Roberts')
sea salt and freshly ground black pepper to taste
4 tablespoons brown sugar
2 litres rich chicken stock
2 tablespoons soy sauce
2 tablespoons Worcestershire sauce
½ cup chopped fresh parsley

Fry the onions in the olive oil until golden, stir frequently. Add the celery and stir-fry for 3 minutes, then add the pumpkin and stir-fry for 1 minute. In a pestle and mortar crush the coriander, cumin and caraway seeds with the lavender flowers and add to the stir-fry pumpkin mixture. Stir well. Now add the rest of the ingredients, except the parsley. Simmer for 30 minutes. Adjust seasoning if necessary. When cooked, whirl in a liquidiser and serve hot with a sprinkling of parsley and crusty brown bread.

COOK'S TIP

In all recipes where pumpkin is an ingredient I love to use the big flat white pumpkin best. You can, however, use any type of pumpkin that you favour, such as butternut, squash, hubbard squash, marrows, susu, and all the new pumpkins that are coming onto the market.

BEETROOT AND LAVENDER SOUP

SERVES 6-8

4 tablespoons olive oil
2 large onions, finely chopped
2 cups chopped celery, leaves included
4 green peppers, chopped (enough to make 3 cups)
2 tablespoons coriander seeds
2 tablespoons caraway seeds
2 tablespoons lavender flowers stripped off their stalks (use L. intermedia var. 'Margaret Roberts')
1 tablespoon freshly grated nutmeg
8-10 medium-sized beetroots, well scrubbed and coarsely grated
3-4 cups chopped beetroot leaves
sea salt and black pepper to taste
2-3 tablespoons soy sauce
juice of 1 lemon
2 litres good strong chicken stock
½ cup chopped fresh mint

Fry the onions in the olive oil until golden. Add the celery, then the green pepper and stir-fry for 3 minutes. Crush the coriander and caraway seeds with the lavender flowers and nutmeg, and add to the stir-fry. Add all the other ingredients except the mint, and simmer for 40 minutes. Whirl in a liquidiser. Serve hot with a sprinkling of chopped mint.

COOK'S TIP

We underestimate the importance of beetroot and carrots in our diet, and it is so satisfying to reap the end-of-summer crop and use it in soups. Both are rich in beta carotene, and vitamins and minerals, and help to lower high blood cholesterol, build good blood cells and act as a tonic on the whole body.

FROM TOP TO BOTTOM: Beetroot and lavender soup; pumpkin and lavender soup; cucumber and lavender soup

Beetroot and apple soup with lavender

Serves 4-6

You can substitute 4 large carrots for the beetroot to ring in the changes.

2 tablespoons olive oil
1 large onion (preferably red), finely chopped
3 apples, peeled, cored and sliced
3 medium-sized potatoes, peeled and diced
4 beetroots, peeled and sliced
1 stick celery, finely chopped
½ teaspoon ground cloves
1 tablespoon fresh lavender flowers stripped off their stems
sea salt and black pepper to taste
1-2 tablespoons horseradish sauce
juice of 1 lemon
chopped parsley

Brown the onions in the olive oil. Add all other ingredients except the horseradish sauce and lemon juice. Add 1½ litres water, and simmer gently until vegetables are tender – about 20 minutes. Adjust the seasoning, then pour into a liquidiser. Whirl until smooth, then add the horseradish sauce and the lemon juice and whirl again. Serve either hot or cold. Decorate with a little chopped parsley.

Cucumber and lavender soup

Serves 4-6

My favourite hot weather soup, this unusually tasty soup is as delicious served chilled.

2 cucumbers, peeled and diced
2 sticks celery, thinly sliced
1 onion, peeled and chopped
1½ litres good stock or water
2 tablespoons cornflour
250 ml plain yoghurt
sea salt and cayenne pepper to taste
juice of 1 lemon
½ cup fresh chopped tarragon
1 tablespoon fresh chopped young lavender leaves
    (L. stoechas Spanish lavender, as used in Spain)
½ tablespoon lavender flowers stripped off their stems
    (L. intermedia var. 'Margaret Roberts')

Boil the cucumbers, celery and onions in the stock or water for about 15 minutes. Liquidise and return to the pot. Mix the cornflour with a little water to a smooth paste and add to the soup mixture. Add the yoghurt, stir well and cook until it thickens. Add the salt, cayenne pepper, lemon juice, tarragon and lavender leaves. Simmer for 2 minutes. Serve piping hot with the lavender flowers sprinkled on top, or chill and serve with a dollop of sour cream in glass bowls on a hot summer evening.

Potato, leek and lavender soup

Serves 6-8

This is a real winter warmer and filling enough to be a meal on its own.

3 tablespoons butter
about 6 leeks, washed well and sliced thinly
6 large potatoes, peeled and diced
4 cups chicken stock
sea salt and black pepper
1 tablespoon young lavender leaves, finely chopped
    (L. intermedia var. 'Grosso' leaves or L. stoechas Spanish lavender leaves)
4 cups milk
chopped parsley
dash of nutmeg

In a large heavy pot, melt the butter and add the leeks. Brown lightly. Add potatoes and coat with the buttery mixture. Stir-fry a minute or two. Add all other ingredients except the milk and simmer until the leeks and potatoes are tender. Liquidise and then return it all to the pot. Add the milk and simmer for 5 minutes. Sprinkle with chopped parsley, a few lavender flowers and a dash of nutmeg. Serve hot with croutons or thick crusty bread.

JERUSALEM ARTICHOKE AND LAVENDER SOUP

SERVES 8

This tasty nutritious soup is a firm favourite in Europe during autumn when the artichokes are plentiful.

500 g fresh Jerusalem artichokes
juice of 2-3 lemons
½ cup sunflower cooking oil
2 large onions, finely chopped
1½ litre chicken stock or water
2 small turnips, peeled and grated
1 tablespoon lavender leaves, finely chopped
   (L. intermedia var. 'Margaret Roberts')
2 tablespoons mint, finely chopped
1 tablespoon fennel seed or stalk and leaves,
   finely chopped
salt and cayenne pepper to taste
150 ml cream

Dice the Jerusalem artichokes, toss in lemon juice to prevent their discolouration and set aside. Meanwhile brown onions in oil. Add the turnips and brown lightly, then add the artichokes to the onion and turnip mixture, and mix together. Add the stock and simmer for 20 minutes or until the artichokes are soft. Liquidise and return to the pot. Add all the other ingredients. (Keep some chopped mint and lavender leaves back for sprinkling on top.) Stir well, and simmer for a further 3-6 minutes. It can be cooled and refrigerated and served chilled, or, serve it hot. Decorate with a mint sprig and a lavender sprig.

CARROT AND LAVENDER SOUP

SERVES 6-8

4 tablespoons olive oil
2 large onions, finely chopped
2 cups chopped celery, leaves included
4 green peppers chopped (enough to make 3 cups)
2 tablespoons coriander seeds
2 tablespoons caraway seeds
2 tablespoons lavender flowers, stripped off their stalks
   (L. intermedia var. 'Margaret Roberts')
1 tablespoon freshly grated nutmeg
8-10 medium-sized carrots, well scrubbed and
   coarsely grated
3-4 cups chopped beetroot leaves
sea salt and black pepper to taste
2-3 tablespoons soy sauce
juice of 1 lemon
2 litres good strong chicken stock
½ cup chopped fresh mint

Fry the onions in the olive oil until golden. Add the celery, then the green peppers and stir-fry for 3 minutes. Crush the coriander and caraway seeds with the lavender flowers and nutmeg, and add to the stir-fry. Add all the other ingredients except the mint and simmer for 40 minutes. Whirl in a liquidiser. Serve hot with a sprinkling of chopped mint.

FISH MAIN DISHES

Lavender in fish dishes is the biggest surprise of all. Chefs all over the country, but particularly in Cape Town, are becoming interested in lavender as a flavour. Whenever I lecture in Cape Town I always spend time showing the young chefs new flavours. Fish with lavender is becoming a firm favourite.

The best lavender to use with fish is L. intermedia var. 'Grosso', and with fishcakes L. intermedia var. 'Margaret Roberts'. But why not try cooking fish with the Spanish lavenders the way the Greeks and Romans did? The fresh taste of lavender lends itself to fish dishes. Once you have tried it, I am sure you will always find yourself reaching for the lavender when preparing fish.

LAVENDER FISH CAKES

SERVES 6

These easy-to-make fish cakes are a favourite with everyone.

sunflower cooking oil
4 cups hake, cooked, skinned, deboned and flaked
2 cups chopped onions
1 cup chopped celery
½ cup chopped parsley
1 cup finely grated carrot
1 cup finely chopped green pepper
2 beaten eggs
sea salt and black pepper to taste
1 tablespoon fresh lavender flowers, stripped off their
*   stems (*L. intermedia *var.* 'Margaret Roberts')
juice of 1 lemon
2 tablespoons cake flour

Heat a large frying pan and add enough sunflower oil to cover the bottom well. Mix all the ingredients together thoroughly. Form into flat cakes, pressing well between your hands. Fry the cakes in the oil until they start to turn golden brown. Carefully lift and flip over with a spatula and fork to fry the other side until golden brown. Get several sheets of kitchen paper towels ready. When the fish cakes are thoroughly cooked through, place on paper towels to absorb excess oil. Keep warm in a serving dish while you fry the rest.

COOK'S TIP

Fish cakes are an ideal way of serving fish, as they taste delicious hot or cold. I make a big batch and keep it in the fridge. It is so convenient to be able to serve home-made fish cakes hot for breakfast with a fried egg and fried tomato slices or cold for lunch with a salad, or hot for dinner with rice, peas and baby carrots, or as a snack or picnic treat between the buttered halves of a fresh bread roll with lettuce and lots of mayonnaise.

LAVENDER AND HAKE STIR-FRY

SERVES 4

a little oil
6 hake fillets, skinned and sliced
1 large onion, thinly sliced
1 green pepper, diced
1 cup thinly sliced cabbage
juice of 1 lemon
2 potatoes, thinly sliced
sea salt and freshly ground black pepper
1 tablespoon finely chopped parsley
2 tablespoons finely chopped fennel leaves
½ tablespoon finely chopped lavender leaves and
*   flowers (*L. intermedia *var.* 'Grosso')

In a frying pan or wok, brown the fish in the oil. Add the onion and green pepper and brown lightly. Add the cabbage, lemon juice and potatoes. Add more oil if necessary. Add the sea salt and pepper. Add the finely chopped parsley, fennel leaves, lavender flowers and lavender leaves. Briskly stir until the potatoes are cooked. Serve hot on brown rice, with fresh lemon wedges. Decorate with a spray or two of lavender flowers and fennel sprigs.

COOK'S TIP

When restaurants in France and Spain serve fruit or fish, they provide bowls of lavender water or lemon verbena in which to rinse your fingers. **Lavender water** is easy to make. Boil 2 cups of lavender sprigs, leaves included, in 5 cups of water for 10 minutes. Stand aside covered and cool. Strain and pour into little finger bowls. Set the bowls at each place setting and place a fresh lavender sprig next to each. This is to rub between the hands to remove fish or onion smells. Remember that lavender is a deodorant. Fresh lemon verbena leaves can be used in the same way.

BAKED FISH WITH LAVENDER SAUCE

SERVES 4-6

This is my favourite quick supper dish when everyone is late and tired. It is quick, easy and appetising.

any fish, skinned and deboned
2 onions, sliced
1 cup chopped celery stalks and leaves
1 cup thinly diced carrots
salt and pepper
some lemon juice

Turn oven to 180 °C. Place the fish in a baking dish. Scatter the onion slices, celery stalks celery leaves and carrots evenly over the fish. Sprinkle with salt, pepper and lemon juice.

SAUCE

2½ cups milk
2 eggs
2 tablespoons cornflour
1 cup grated cheese
1 tablespoon chopped lavender leaves (L. stoechas Spanish lavender – my favourite is 'Avonview' – new name 'After Midnight')
chopped parsley for sprinkling on top

Whisk the milk with the eggs and cornflour. Add the grated cheese and stir in well. Pour over the fish. Sprinkle with the chopped lavender leaves. Bake at 180 °C for 20-25 minutes or until lightly brown on top and bubbly. Sprinkle with the chopped parsley. Serve piping hot with mashed potato and a salad.

BRAAIED FISH WITH LAVENDER AND ROSEMARY

SERVES 4-6

6-8 fish fillets
2 peeled apples, quartered
2 onions, thinly sliced
1 sprig lavender (L. intermedia var. 'Margaret Roberts')
1 sprig rosemary
1 tablespoon crushed coriander seeds
sea salt and black pepper to taste
2 tablespoons butter
fresh lemon juice

Place the fish in a large double piece of tin foil. Arrange the apples, onions, lavender, rosemary and coriander seeds all around on top of the fish. Sprinkle with sea salt and black pepper. Dot with butter and squeeze the lemon juice over everything. Fold up well and place over the glowing coals. Tuck in well-scrubbed potatoes to bake with the fish in the coals. When the potatoes are done, the fish will be done. Turn the parcel over from time to time to cook evenly on the coals. Discard the rosemary and lavender sprigs for serving. Serve piping hot. Add a squeeze of lemon juice and a pat of butter to the baked potatoes.

COOK'S TIP

Braaied fish is most delicious when you use a whole fish that has been freshly caught, cleaned and trimmed, or big filleted pieces, even braai the head – it is considered to be a delicacy – and be generous with the lemon juice.

Surprisingly tasty and extra nourishing, this baked fish with lavender sauce is a favourite supper dish with everyone. Enjoy!

TUNA AND LAVENDER LUNCH DISH

SERVES 4

This quick and easy dish is a tasty standby.

1 tin tuna in brine
1 tablespoon fresh lavender flowers, stripped off their
   stems (L. intermedia *var. 'Margaret Roberts'*)
¾ cup good mayonnaise
¾ cup finely chopped celery
1 green pepper, finely chopped
¾ cup spring onions, finely chopped
sea salt and black pepper
juice of 1 lemon

Drain the tuna and then mash it thoroughly. Add the lavender flowers to the mayonnaise, then mix it into the tuna. Add all the other ingredients and mix well. Serve on a bed of lettuce with a squeeze of lemon juice and a sprinkling of chopped parsley.

MEAT AND CHICKEN MAIN DISHES

Lavender is extremely beneficial for gastric ailments, particularly flatulence, and helps to tenderise tough meat. It seems to be a natural choice as an ingredient in casseroles, stews and braised meat dishes. The antispasmodic properties in lavender help to break down and digest fatty meats and it has the wonderful ability to assist the liver in its processing. With these remarkable properties, lavender surely deserves more recognition as an important culinary herb.

LAVENDER MEAT LOAF

SERVES 6-8

This is one of my favourite standby dishes – everyone loves it! It tastes so good and is so quick and easy to make that you will find yourself serving it at dinner parties.

1 tablespoon crushed cumin seeds
2 teaspoons crushed cardamom seed, hard
   dry husk removed
1-2 teaspoons cayenne pepper
3-4 teaspoons coarse sea salt
½ cup fruit chutney (optional)
½ cup good tomato sauce (optional)
500 g minced topside
3 cups finely grated carrots
3 cups finely chopped onions
3 cups peeled chopped tomatoes
2 cups finely chopped celery
2 cups finely chopped green peppers
2 tablespoons fresh thyme, stripped off its stalks
1 tablespoon lavender flowers, stripped off their stalks
   (L. intermedia *var. 'Margaret Roberts'*)
juice of 1 lemon
2 teaspoons lemon zest
2 beaten eggs
potatoes and onions for roasting (enough for 6-8)
a little sunflower oil

Pound the cumin seeds, cardamom seed, cayenne pepper and sea salt together. Mix all the ingredients together, except the potatoes and onions. Add ½ cup fruit chutney for extra flavour (optional) and ½ cup good tomato sauce (optional) at this point. Mix well with the hands, literally squeeze it all into the mixture. Grease a large flat baking dish. Pack mixture into baking dish, patting and shaping firmly to make a loaf about 5 cm high. Peel the potatoes, peel and halve the onions and pack around the sides of the meat loaf. Dribble a little sunflower oil over the loaf and vegetables. Add a little salt to the vegetables and bake at 180 °C for 1 hour. Baste the loaf occasionally and check with a fork to see whether it is thoroughly cooked inside. Serve piping hot with peas or green beans and rice.

COOK'S TIP

The lavender meat loaf (see previous page) is a hands-on recipe, so scrub up well, roll your sleeves up and get stuck in. Use a baking dish big enough to pack in the meat loaf and roast potatoes and onions along the sides. I sometimes substitute the onion and potatoes with pumpkin slices and sweet potatoes to ring the changes.

BEEF AND LAVENDER CASSEROLE

SERVES 6

This is a wonderfully nourishing stanby dish, my son's favourite meal, so I make it whenever he visits. Substantially sticking to the ribs, no one ever tires of it.

2 large onions, sliced
a little cooking oil
1 kg thinly sliced rump steak
2 tablespoons flour
2 celery sticks, sliced
6 carrots, peeled and diced
2 green peppers, sliced
4 large tomatoes, peeled and sliced
4 large potatoes, peeled and diced
sea salt and cayenne pepper to taste
2 tablespoons brown sugar
1 tablespoon fresh thyme
1 tablespoon freshly chopped lavender leaves
  (L. stoechas, Spanish lavender)
2 teaspoons coriander seeds, crushed
juice of 1 lemon

Brown the onions in oil in a large heavy iron pot. Roll the meat in flour, then add to the pot and brown. Add all the other ingredients and enough water to cover. Stir well as the mixture starts to boil, then cover with a lid. Either simmer on the stove-top, or bake in a hot oven (180 °C) until tender. Stir occasionally and add a little water if necessary. Serve with brown rice and green beans.

PORK CHOPS BRAAIED WITH LAVENDER AND HONEY

SERVES 4

4 pork chops trimmed of excess fat
salt and cayenne pepper to taste
juice of 2 lemons
1 tablespoon freshly chopped lavender leaves
  (L. stoechas Spanish lavender)
3 tablespoons honey
pinch of cloves
sprinkle of fennel seed

Mix all the ingredients except the meat together like a marinade. Pour into a screw-top jar and shake. Pour over the chops and turn them in it. Leave in the fridge overnight. Next day place everything in a roasting pan and grill either in the oven or over the coals. Baste frequently until the chops are golden and tender. Serve with grilled tomatoes, mashed potato and green peas.

TOP: Pork chops braaied with lavender and honey
RIGHT: Mutton hot pot with lavender

MUTTON HOT POT WITH LAVENDER

SERVES 6

This is a wonderfully nourishing standby dish, which can be kept in the fridge and reheated when necessary.

12 small mutton loin chops
2 large onions, peeled and sliced
oil for browning chops
2 cups sliced green beans
2 green peppers, seeded and chopped
1 cup lentils, soaked in water for 10 minutes
1 cup diced mushrooms
sea salt and cayenne pepper to taste
4 large potatoes, peeled and cubed
about 1 litre water
juice of 1 lemon
2 sprigs lavender (L. intermedia *var.* 'Margaret Roberts')
1 sprig rosemary
4 carrots, peeled and diced
2-3 tablespoons flour, to thicken gravy if necessary

In a large heavy-bottomed pot brown the chops and the onions in the oil. Add all the other ingredients. Toss lightly to separate ingredients – some will brown a little more. Add enough water to cover the mixture. If necessary, 2-3 tablespoons flour can be mixed with water to thicken the gravy. Simmer gently. Stir occasionally and add more water if needed. Adjust the flavouring and remove the lavender and rosemary sprigs just before serving. Serve with brown rice and a salad.

LAVENDER CHICKEN BREASTS

SERVES 4-6

This easily-made dish is bound to become a firm favourite.

4 large chicken breasts, cut in half lengthways
2 onions, cut into rings
2 cups coarse brown breadcrumbs
1 cup chopped celery
1 cup plain yoghurt
a little butter
juice of 1 lemon
1 tablespoon Brewer's yeast or Mega yeast (Vital Health Foods)
1 tablespoon fresh thyme leaves
sea salt and cayenne pepper to taste
½ tablespoon chopped fresh lavender leaves (traditionally L. stoechas *Spanish lavender*)

Lay the chicken breasts in a baking dish and cover with onion rings. Mix the breadcrumbs, celery and yoghurt first then add all the other ingredients and stir well, and spoon mixture over the chicken breasts. Dot with butter and bake covered until tender, about 25 minutes. Remove the cover and brown lightly under the grill. Serve hot with baked potatoes and peas.

COOKS'S TIP

Poultry tastes extra rich and succulent when cooked with fresh lavender, and pieces of chicken can be marinated in the yoghurt sauce and left in the fridge overnight. This method will add extra flavour to the dish.

Chicken and lavender stir-fry

Serves 4-6
Quick, easy and delicious, and loved by everyone I can make it in 10 minutes. All sorts of ingredients can be added to ring in the changes.

olive oil
2 onions, finely chopped
6 chicken breasts cut into cubes (I buy the deboned breasts and keep it in the deep freeze but you can substitute breasts for chicken thighs)
1½ cups chopped green pepper
1 cup chopped celery
2 tablespoons grated fresh ginger
2 cups mushrooms, thinly sliced
juice of 1 lemon
1 tablespoon coriander seed, crushed
1 tablespoon fennel seed, crushed
sea salt and black pepper to taste
½ tablespoon lavender flowers stripped off their stalks (use L. intermedia *var. 'Margaret Roberts')*
3-4 tablespoons sesame seeds
water or chicken stock

I use a wok or a large frying pan. Brown the onions in the olive oil, then add the chicken pieces and brown, stirring all the time. Next add the green peppers followed by the celery and the grated ginger, then add the mushrooms. Add a dash of olive oil and stir-fry vigorously. Now add the lemon juice, the spices, the salt and pepper, the lavender flowers and the sesame seed. Stir-fry well and finally add a little water or chicken stock, simmer for a minute with the lid on and stir-fry. The smell will be tantalising. Have ready a bed of rice, tip the pan's content onto it and serve piping hot with a wedge of lemon and a fresh green salad.

Vegetarian dishes

Lavender lends itself to pulses and pastas as it is so refreshing and an excellent digestive. Lavender is important in the cuisine of the future. Cooking for health is paramount, and the gentle antispasmodic properties in lavender soothe the whole digestive tract.

Stuffed marrow with lavender

Serves 6
2 cups sliced mushrooms
a little oil
salt and pepper to taste
1 tablespoon freshly chopped lavender leaves (L. stoechas Spanish lavender or use 'Avonview' – now called 'After Midnight')
2 cups brown bread crumbs
2 onions, finely chopped
cayenne pepper
1 medium-sized summer squash
2 tablespoons skimmed milk powder
a little lemon juice
potatoes and carrots to accompany the stuffed marrow
a little butter

Sauté the mushrooms in a little oil with the salt, pepper and lavender leaves. Add the breadcrumbs and sauté, then add the onions and sauté stirring well. Season with salt and cayenne pepper. Cut off one end of a summer squash and remove the pips. Stuff the hollow of the squash with the mushroom mixture and the skim-milk powder, and a good squeeze of lemon juice over the top. Prop the end in place with toothpicks. Place in a baking tray. Peel the potatoes and carrots and place in the baking tray with the stuffed marrow. Dot with a little butter and tuck a lavender sprig under the squash. Cover and roast until tender. Serve hot, sliced on a bed of brown rice and peas.

Lavender pasta with lavender, melissa and grenadilla unwinder drink

LAVENDER AND BUTTER BEAN PIE

SERVES 6-8

This is a favourite Provence recipe and keeps well in the fridge.

1 kg butter beans, soaked overnight and washed
½ kg potatoes
butter (for mashed potatoes)
salt and pepper
2 onions, sliced into rings
a little oil
1 teaspoon Marmite
200 g grated cheese (2 cups)
a little milk and 1 beaten egg, whisked together
1 tablespoon chopped lavender leaves (L. intermedia
'Grosso', as used in France)

Boil the beans in water until tender, about 1 hour. Cook the potatoes and mash with the butter, salt and pepper and egg and milk mixture. Sauté the onions in oil until lightly browned. Spoon a layer of the beans and the onions into an ovenproof dish. Dissolve the Marmite in a little hot water, about 150 ml. Pour over the beans and top with half the cheese. Spread the mashed potatoes over the mixture and sprinkle with the chopped lavender, then the rest of the cheese. Dot with butter and bake at 180 °C for 20 minutes or until golden.

COOK'S TIP

This filling dish sticks to the ribs. The lavender and mint help with flatulence, and the gasiness of the beans is removed by discarding the first water. Boil up the beans and cook for 5 minutes, then drain and discard the water, and boil up again in fresh water.

LAVENDER PASTA

SERVES 6

This recipe was given to me by an Italian chef some years ago and I make it today with as much pleasure as I did then.

1 litre milk
1 finely chopped onion
2 finely grated carrots
½ tablespoon chopped fresh lavender leaves
    (L. stoechas Spanish lavender)
2 tablespoons cornflour, mixed with a little milk
2 beaten eggs
2 teaspoons mustard powder
pasta (for 6)
2 cups grated cheese
1 tablespoon chopped parsley
salt and pepper to taste

Boil the milk with the onion, carrots and the lavender leaves for 10 minutes. Add a little more milk if necessary. Whisk the cornflour, beaten eggs and mustard powder together, and boil with the milk mixture until it thickens, stirring all the time. Fold in half the cheese. Cook the pasta. Pour the sauce over the hot pasta, sprinkle with the other half of the cheese and top with the chopped parsley and a lavender flowerstalk or two.

LAVENDER RICE DISH

SERVES 4-6

A friend, who was a chef in Provence a few years ago, was given this delectable rather Italian recipe by the French chefs there and he makes it frequently in the restaurant in his hometown of Durban and it's always a success.

1 kg broccoli
1 large onion, diced
1 clove garlic, crushed
knob of butter
sea salt and freshly ground black pepper
2 teaspoons freshly chopped lavender leaves
  (L. intermedia var. 'Grosso' or L. stoechas Spanish
  lavender – I usually use 'After Midnight')
2 cups cooked brown rice or risotto rice
a sprinkling of breadcrumbs
a little mozzarella cheese

Wash and shred the broccoli. Place in a pot in a little water with the onion, garlic, a knob of butter, salt, pepper and lavender leaves. Cover and cook till tender, about 6-7 minutes. Pour the vegetables into an ovenproof dish. Add the cooked rice. Pour the sauce (see below) over the vegetables and sprinkle with breadcrumbs and a little grated mozzarella cheese. Dot with butter and bake at 180 °C for 15-20 minutes. Serve with a salad and baked potatoes.

SAUCE

2 tablespoons butter
2 tablespoons flour
2 beaten eggs
salt and pepper
2-3 tablespoons tomato paste
400 ml vegetable stock or milk

Melt the butter, add the flour, stir well and set aside. Add the eggs, salt, pepper and tomato paste to the vegetable stock or milk. Add this liquid to the butter and flour mixture. Stir as it begins to thicken. Pour hot over the pasta and stir gently.

COOK'S TIP

My friend said that the Provencal chefs varied this lavender rice dish weekly with whatever greens were in season, even using combinations of some. Other greens that work well in this dish are kale, leeks, spinach, courgettes and beetroot tops.

MUSHROOM AND LAVENDER BAKE

SERVES 6

Feel like something different? This tasty dish is not only delicious but so easy to make!

some olive oil
2 cloves garlic, peeled and thinly sliced
2 tablespoons butter
10 medium-sized potatoes, peeled and sliced
1 punnet brown mushrooms sliced
2 large onions, thinly sliced
sea salt and freshly ground black pepper
1 tablespoon finely chopped lavender leaves
  (L. intermedia var. 'Margaret Roberts')
2 tablespoons crushed coriander
1 tablespoon crushed fennel seed
2 tablespoons finely chopped mint
1 cup grated mozzarella cheese
2 cups cream
2 cups milk

Preheat oven to 180 °C. Grease the bottom of a large baking dish with olive oil and scatter the chopped garlic into the dish. Layer the potatoes, mushrooms, onions, salt, pepper and the lavender leaves, coriander, fennel seed and mint. Continue layering until all the ingredients are used up, finishing with a layer of potatoes. Whisk the cream and milk together, and pour over layered ingredients. Make sure that the top layer of potatoes is properly covered with the cream and milk mixture. Dot with butter. Bake uncovered for about 1 hour or until the potatoes are tender, crisp and golden. Serve hot with a salad.

LAVENDER, CHICKPEA AND GREEN BEAN SALAD

SERVES 6-10

This wonderful standby can be served hot or cold and keeps for a long time in the fridge.

500 g chickpeas, soaked
500 g green beans, chopped and topped and tailed
1½-2 cups soft brown caramel sugar
3 cups brown grape vinegar
2 tablespoons crushed coriander seed
1 cup mint, finely chopped
2 tablespoons lavender flowers, stripped off their stalks
   (L. intermedia var. 'Margaret Roberts')
2 cups celery, finely chopped
sea salt and freshly ground black pepper

Cook the chickpeas until they are tender and then drain. Cook the green beans until they are tender and then drain. Mix the sugar into the vinegar with the coriander seed, mint and lavender flowers. Let it all stand for 1 hour. Mix every now and then to dissolve the sugar and draw the flavours out. Add the celery, and season with salt and pepper. Store in a sealed dish in the fridge. Serve with toasted Italian bread and a little dribble of olive oil, or as a salad with cold chicken and ham.

DESSERTS

Here lavender really excels, that fragrant fresh palate-cleansing taste lends itself to beautiful desserts. I would say that to really do justice to a meal try lavender tea.

LAVENDER TEA

SERVES 1

1 cup boiling water
¼ cup fresh leaves and flowers of L. intermedia var. 'Margaret Roberts'

Boil the water and pour over the leaves and flowers. Let it stand for 5 minutes, then strain. Sip slowly.

COOK'S TIP

A few sips of lavender tea between courses will enhance every dish that follows. The taste buds will literally sparkle with the freshness that lavender imparts.

LAVENDER SUGAR

about 750 g sugar
4 or 6 sprays of flowers and leaves (L. intermedia var. 'Grosso' or 'Margaret Roberts')

Pour the sugar into a jar. Press 4 or 6 sprays of fresh lavender flowers and leaves into the jar so that the sugar completely covers them. Keep the jar sealed for 1 week, then shake out and discard the old sprigs, and add fresh sprigs. Seal the jar for another week. By now the sugar should be fragrant with lavender and completely laced with its stunning flavour. However, if this is not strong enough for you, then simply repeat the process.

When fresh lavender flowers are pressed into sugar, the sugar takes on the fragrance and taste of the lavender. This sugar can then be used for baking or cooking with lavender. It can also be used for drinks, syrups and crystallised fruits. Fresh lavender flowers can also be pressed into icing sugar and castor sugar.

LAVENDER HONEY

Lavender honey is a great favourite. I always have a good quantity on hand.

500 g bottle fresh honey (before it has solidified)
1 cup lavender flowers and leafy sprigs
*   (L. intermedia var. 'Grosso')*

Push the lavender flowers and sprigs into the honey. Stand the jar in a pot of hot water (not boiling) to infuse the oils of the lavender into the honey for about 20 minutes. Store for a month before using, then strain the honey and discard the flowers and leaves. I often leave a flower stem in the honey for quick identification on the kitchen shelf.

COOK'S TIP

Lavender honey is a great-tasting healthy sweetener for herb teas, cool drinks and fruit punches. It is also an excellent natural remedy for soothing those tiresome winter coughs and sore throats. Add 2 teaspoons of the honey to a cup of boiling water with a slice of lemon and a good squeeze of lemon juice. Even a dash of sherry or brandy could be added to make a powerful cough soother.

You could also add ¼ cup of sage leaves, or 2 or 3 cloves, to the boiling water for a superb cough and cold mixture.

LAVENDER FRUIT SALAD

SERVES 4-6
Refreshingly, revivingly enticing, this quick fruit salad can vary with whatever fruit is in season.

about 4 cups mixed fresh fruit, like mangoes, peaches,
*   pawpaw, apples, bananas, strawberries*
grenadilla pulp
1 cup mango or litchi juice
2 sprigs lavender (L. intermedia var. 'Margaret
*   Roberts')*
lavender sugar or lavender honey (see recipes above)
tender young lavender flowers, stripped off their stalks
*   (L. intermedia var. 'Margaret Roberts')*

Cut the fruit into the bowl and add the grenadilla pulp. Warm 1 cup of mango or litchi juice with 2 sprigs of lavender for 5 minutes. Discard the lavender sprigs and pour the juice over the fruit. Sprinkle the lavender flowers over the whole fruit salad. Serve with lavender sprigs tucked under the bowl or on the saucer of each individual dessert dish.

COOK'S TIP

My absolute favourite fruits in a fruit salad are green honeydew melon made into balls, sliced fresh peaches and mangoes and strawberries cut into halves. Sprinkle very tart fruit with lavender sugar or lavender honey before mixing into the fruit salad.

Top: Lemon and lavender tart
Left: Strawberry and lavender cheesecake

LAVENDER MERINGUES

MAKES ABOUT 24 MERINGUES

6 egg whites
3 tablespoons fresh lavender flowers (L. intermedia
  var. 'Grosso' or 'Margaret Roberts')
3 tablespoons castor sugar
275 g white sugar
4 teaspoons baking powder

In a clean bowl beat the egg whites until they are stiff. In another bowl, crush the lavender flowers with the castor sugar, then add the white sugar. Add the baking powder and stir until well mixed. Fold in gently and lightly to the beaten egg whites, a little at a time. Cover a baking tray with double folded brown paper. Place meringue mixture, a tablespoon at a time in rows onto the baking tray at least 3 cm apart. Bake overnight in a cool oven, 100 °C. I usually switch the oven off for the last 3-4 hours. They need about 10-12 hours to dry out. Sandwich the meringues together with lavender cream and serve on a pretty plate decorated with lavender flowers, and a cup of lavender tea.

LAVENDER CREAM

250 ml fresh cream
1 tablespoon fresh lavender flowers (L. intermedia var.
  'Grosso' or 'Margaret Roberts')
3 tablespoons castor sugar

Whisk the cream until thick. Add the lavender flowers and castor sugar.

LEMON AND LAVENDER TART

SERVES 6

I serve this refreshing light tart often, as it is foolproof, quick and easy:

PASTRY

125 g wholewheat flour
85 g butter
pinch of salt

Sift the flour into a large bowl and grate in the butter on a coarse grater. Add salt and rub briefly together until a soft dough is formed. Pat out into a 20 cm baking dish, pressing dough up the sides a little. Bake at 180 °C until lightly golden and crisp, about 10 minutes.

FILLING

about 3 teaspoons grated lemon rind
3 large lemons
3 eggs
150 g castor sugar
150 ml cream
2 sprigs lavender flowers, stripped off their stalks to
  equal 1 tablespoon (use L. intermedia 'Grosso')

Grate the lemon rind into a bowl. Squeeze the lemons and mix the juice with the rind. Beat the eggs and castor sugar. Add the cream and whisk until smooth. Add to the lemon juice and rind. Whisk until smooth. Add the lavender flowers last. Pour into the pastry case and bake at 140 °C for about 40 minutes or until firm. Serve chilled with whipped cream decorated with lavender flowers.

STRAWBERRY AND LAVENDER CHEESECAKE

SERVES 6-8
This is a real party piece!

CRUST

1 packet plain digestive biscuits
175 g butter
oil

Crush the biscuits with a rolling pin. Melt the butter in a saucepan and mix well with the biscuits. Line a 20 cm loose-based cake tin with greaseproof paper, and oil well. Press the biscuit mixture evenly into the cake tin. Chill.

FILLING

175 g castor sugar
2 teaspoons vanilla
3 eggs separated
juice and rind of 1 lemon
*1 tablespoon fresh lavender flowers, stripped off their
    stems (*L. intermedia *var. 'Grosso')*
500 g chunky plain cream cheese
150 ml thick cream

Whisk the castor sugar, vanilla and egg yolks. Mix in the lemon juice, rind, lavender flowers and cream cheese. Whisk the cream and, in another bowl, whisk the egg whites. Fold the cream and then the egg whites into the cream cheese mixture, gently using a metal spoon. Pour into the chilled biscuit base. Bake at 140 °C for 40-60 minutes or until it is set. Set aside to cool.

TOPPING

3 cups strawberries
slices of kiwi fruit
a little brown sugar
1 cup red currant jelly

Slice the strawberries and kiwi fruit. Sprinkle with a little brown sugar. When the cake is cool, pack the strawberries and kiwi fruit in circles on top. Melt the red currant jelly in a saucepan and gently pour over strawberries and kiwi fruit to make a glaze. Serve cool with a sprig or two of lavender across the top.

COOK'S TIP

Instead of strawberries you can use peaches, stewed apples, gooseberries or grated pineapple or whatever fruit is in season, you can even combine fruits.

LAVENDER ICE-CREAM

SERVES 6-8
500 ml milk
*2 tablespoons fresh lavender flowers (*L. intermedia
    var. 'Grosso')
2 eggs
250 g castor sugar
2 tablespoons cornflour mixed with a little milk
2 full cups thick cream, well beaten

Warm the milk and the lavender flowers in a saucepan. Beat the eggs with the castor sugar until creamy, then add the cornflour. Add to the milk and lavender flower mixture slowly and carefully, beating all the time with a wooden spoon. Once the mixture has thickened, let it stand covered and cool. Fold in the cream and pour into freezer trays. Leave in the freezer for 1 hour. Remove from freezer, spoon into a large bowl, beat well, refill the freezer trays and return to freezer. Do this once or twice more, then freeze until firm. Beating the mixture up well breaks down slatey ice crystals and makes it light and spongy. Serve in glass bowls with lavender sprigs and lavender shortbread in the saucer.

COOK'S TIP

Try adding a little touch of mauve food colouring to this exquisite ice-cream. I did it for a dinner party, and served it decorated with fresh lavender sprigs and accompanied by lavender shortbread. My guests have never forgotten it. They called it 'food for the soul'!

LAVENDER AND ORANGE JELLY

SERVES 6

This was my children's favourite when they were little. I always had it as a winter treat, for picnics or for lunches in the sun when oranges were plentiful in July.

Lavender and orange jelly set in the orange skins.

2 eggs
1 cup sugar
3 tablespoons gelatine
½ cup warm water
juice of 6-8 oranges – save the skins
3 teaspoons orange rind
2 teaspoons lavender flowers (L. intermedia *var.* 'Margaret Roberts)

Beat the eggs with the sugar until white and foamy. Mix the gelatine with the warm water until dissolved. Mix all the ingredients together. Pour into a glass dish or into the orange skins and place in the fridge to set.

COOK'S TIP

Instead of setting the jelly in a glass dish, pour it into the empty orange skins that you cut in half and squeezed out. This is an excellent picnic treat as children just peel away the skin and eat the jelly.

RHUBARB AND LAVENDER CRUMBLE

SERVES 6-8

This is a wonderful dessert for Sunday lunch.

750 g fresh rhubarb stalks
1 cup castor sugar

Preheat oven to 180 °C. Chop the rhubarb stalks to 2 cm lengths. Arrange the rhubarb in a level layer in a baking dish about 20 cm in diameter. Sprinkle with the castor sugar.

TOPPING

140 g flour
1 tablespoon fresh lavender flowers (L. intermedia *var.* 'Margaret Roberts')
5 tablespoons castor sugar
125 g soft butter
pinch of salt

Combine all the ingredients and rub lightly with fingertips until the mixture resembles coarse bread-crumbs. Work quickly and lightly. Sprinkle over the rhubarb and bake in the centre of the oven for 45 minutes or until the rhubarb is soft. Serve warm with fresh cream.

LAVENDER AND ROSE SORBET

SERVES 6

300 ml water

250 g castor sugar

1 cup rose petals (unsprayed)

1 tablespoon fresh lavender flowers, stripped off their
*   stems (L. intermedia var. 'Margaret Roberts')*

juice of 1 lemon

In a pot heat the water, sugar, rose petals and lavender flowers. Dissolve the sugar and stir gently. Boil for 5 minutes to form a syrup, then remove from the heat and cool. Strain. Add the lemon juice to the syrup, pour into an ice-cream tray and freeze uncovered. Stir often to break up ice crystals, or if you are in a rush freeze until solid without stirring for at least 6 hours or overnight. The next day cut into small chunks and whirl in a food processor until soft and fluffy. Return to the container and freeze again. Serve in scoops straight from the freezer, decorated with rose petals and lavender.

BACK: Lavender ice-cream with lavender praline
RIGHT: Lavender milkshake (page 114)
FRONT: Lavender and rose sorbet

COOK'S TIP

The petals of the Crimson Glory rose are beautifully fragrant and delicious to eat, or you can use any unsprayed roses. The shell pink Margaret Roberts rose, an old-fashioned apothecary rose, has particularly tender petals that make an exquisite ice-cream.

LAVENDER PRALINE

200 g castor sugar

2 tablespoons fresh lavender flowers stripped off
*   their stems (use L. intermedia var. 'Grosso' or*
*   'Margaret Roberts')*

Mix the castor sugar and the lavender flowers together in a heavy-bottomed pot, stirring as the mixture heats up. Keep moving it around as it starts to melt. Keep heat on medium. When mixture is light brown and caramelised, pour onto a well-greased, papered tray in a thin stream, or into greased moulds, or into drops. Cool. Crush into shards or fine pieces and sprinkle onto desserts, especially lavender ice-cream. Or serve as a sweet with after-dinner coffee.

COOK'S TIP

This lavender praline makes a fabulous cake and ice-cream topping or it can be enjoyed in chunks as a delicious sweet. As a sweet it can be made into little caramel drops by spooning a little onto a grease-proof paper lined tray. I always make this at Easter, when I add chopped pecan nuts with the lavender and pour it into little greased moulds for visiting children.

BAKING WITH LAVENDER

Lavender breads, scones and biscuits are delicious. Simply add a tablespoon of lavender flowers to your favourite recipe! In all these recipes I have found that either L. intermedia 'Grosso' or 'Margaret Roberts' is best.

LAVENDER OIL SCONES

MAKES A DOZEN LARGE SCONES
This recipe was given to me by a beloved French teacher who lived in Montpellier, France. She gathered the lavender from the hillsides and used it fresh.

500 g cake flour and wholewheat flour mixed
4 teaspoons baking powder
½ teaspoon salt
1 tablespoon lavender flowers (L. intermedia var. 'Grosso')
2 eggs
100 ml milk
100 ml sunflower cooking oil

Mix the flour, baking powder, salt and lavender flowers. Beat the eggs with the milk. Beat the oil into the milk and egg mixture. With a knife, cut the egg mixture into the flour mixture until it all combines, but do not knead. Drop spoonfuls about 3 cm apart onto a greased baking tray. Bake at 220 °C for 10 minutes or just as scones start to turn golden. Serve hot split open with butter and lavender honey.

LAVENDER CRUMPETS

MAKES AROUND 24 CRUMPETS
Served hot for Sunday morning tea these easy-to-make treats are a pleasure!

500 ml cake flour
4 teaspoons baking powder
pinch of salt
3 eggs, beaten
4 tablespoons sugar
250 ml milk
½ teaspoon fresh lavender flowers (L. intermedia var. 'Margaret Roberts')
2 tablespoons soft butter

Sift the flour, baking powder and salt twice into a bowl. Whisk the eggs and the sugar until light and foamy, then add the milk, lavender flowers and butter. Whisk well, add to the flour mixture and beat until there are no lumps and mixture forms a smooth batter. Heat a griddle or pan and oil it well. Drop the mixture, one tablespoon at a time, onto the hot griddle or pan. Watch until the mixture bubbles, then flip it over with a spatula. Serve hot with butter and jam or lavender honey. For a real treat serve with whipped cream and fresh strawberries.

LAVENDER LOAF

MAKES 1 LARGE LOAF OR 4-6 LITTLE LOAVES
I bake this quick and appealing loaf often and serve it in small flowerpots or little individual loaf pans.

500 g wholewheat flour
3 teaspoons baking powder
1 teaspoon salt
½ cup sunflower seeds
1 tablespoon fresh lavender flowers (L. intermedia var. 'Grosso' or 'Margaret Roberts')
125 ml milk
2 tablespoons honey
500 ml plain yoghurt

Mix the flour, baking powder, salt, sunflower seeds and lavender flowers. Warm the milk, honey and yoghurt together, add to the flour mixture, stir thoroughly, and pour into a well-greased pan or lined flowerpots. Bake at 180 °C for 30-40 minutes or until the loaf sounds hollow when tapped. The little loaf pans take a shorter time – about 20 minutes. Serve wrapped in a warm kitchen towel with a little bunch of lavender tucked in, and lavender butter.

Individual lavender loaves

Cream the butter and castor sugar briskly until light and fluffy. Mix the lavender flowers, cornflour and cake flour and stir in gradually to the buttery mixture. Mix well with fingertips to form a smooth, stiff dough. Press into a baking tray about 2 cm thick. Prick with a fork. Bake at 150 °C until firm and lightly gold in colour. Dredge with castor sugar and cut into squares while still hot. Serve on a plate with lavender flowers all round it, with afternoon tea, and think of your grandmother. This shortbread keeps well in an airtight tin.

LAVENDER BUTTER

1 cup butter
1 tablespoon parsley, chopped
1 tablespoon fresh lavender flowers (L. intermedia
  var. 'Grosso')
pinch salt

Mash the butter with the parsley and the lavender flowers. Add a pinch of salt and smear into little individual pots.

LAVENDER SHORTBREAD

SERVES 6-8
250 g soft butter
75 ml castor sugar
2 tablespoons lavender flowers (L. intermedia var.
  'Grosso')
30 ml cornflour
750 ml cake flour

LAVENDER CRUNCHIES

MAKES ABOUT 20 CRUNCHIES
These tuck-box treats are every schoolchild's favourite!

1 cup cake flour
2 cups oats
2 cups coconut
1 cup brown sugar
2 teaspoons cinnamon
1 tablespoon lavender flowers (L. intermedia var.
  'Margaret Roberts')
60 ml golden syrup
1½ cups butter
2 teaspoons bicarbonate of soda
60 ml milk

Mix the cake flour, oats, coconut, sugar, cinnamon and lavender flowers. Melt the butter with the golden syrup and add to the dry ingredients. Mix the bicarbonate of soda and the milk, and stir into the mixture. Stir thoroughly. Spoon into a greased baking tray and press down well. Bake at 180 °C for 15-20 minutes. Cut into squares while still hot, lift out and cool on wire cake coolers. The crunchies keep well in a sealed tin.

FOR THE CONNOISSEUR

LAVENDER POLLEN

Once or twice I have come across the words 'Lavender pollen' in old recipes. I discovered only recently that this is the name given to crushed or ground lavender. As the recipes come from England, this will be ground Lavandula angustifolia, *and we can safely substitute* L. intermedia *'Grosso'.*

Crushed dried lavender flowers stripped off their stems can be pounded in a pestle and mortar or whirled in a food processor until they are finely ground down. A little of this fine and fragrant powder can be added to hand cream, shampoo, talc powder and bath soaps. Liquid soap is lovely with a little lavender pollen mixed into it. It can also be added to scone dough, pancake batter, pasta dishes, cheese spreads, salad dressings, syrups, cordials, jams, preserves, custards, yoghurts, and whipped cream.

It is potent, so only add a little at a time to try out. But isn't it an exciting thought? Try lavender pollen for something different. Store in a glass jar with a good screw-top lid.

LAVENDER VINEGAR

This easy-to-make refreshing vinegar is delicious in salads, stir-fries, with fish, pasta and potato chips. Use a white-grape vinegar or apple cider vinegar as a base, and because of the fragrant oils you need only make one extraction.

1 bottle white-grape vinegar
6-8 sprigs of lavender flowers

Push the sprigs of lavender flowers into a bottle of white-grape vinegar. Place the bottle in the sun for 1 week. Turn and shake daily. When the week is up strain out the lavender, decant the now fragrant vinegar into a new decorative bottle, and add one or two lavender flowers. Label and date.

HERBES DE PROVENÇE

You can create your own house blend of Herbs of Provençe, which will give your cooking that distinctive different taste. This is my secret recipe.

2 tablespoons dried oregano
3 tablespoons dried thyme
1 tablespoon dried winter savory
*1 tablespoon dried lavender flowers (*L. intermedia *var. 'Margaret Roberts')*
1 tablespoon dried rosemary
2 tablespoons dried chopped celery

Mix herbs well and keep in a screw-top jar near the stove or tie into little bundles made of cheesecloth to get the taste but not the texture.

COOK'S TIP

Use Herbes de Provençe in casseroles, soups, stews, stir-fries. It is particularly delicious with grilled fish, chicken and big black mushrooms. In winter I add 2 tablespoons celery seed to give it a different taste in soups.

LAVENDER LIQUEUR

MAKES ABOUT 1½ LITRES

This drink is superb as an after-dinner liqueur, especially in winter. It can also be served over steamed puddings or baked custard.

6 large sweet oranges
1 litre brandy
2 cups sugar
1 tablespoon lavender flowers (L. intermedia var. 'Grosso')

Grate off the orange rind with a fine grater. Squeeze out the orange juice, and pour into a large jar with a screw top. Mix the brandy and the sugar together, and add the grated zest and lavender flowers. Seal well. Shake the jar well and leave to infuse for no less than 6 weeks. Give it the odd shake during that time. When it is ready strain through a piece of cheesecloth and pour into a pretty decanter.

LAVENDER SYRUP

MAKES 1 LARGE BOTTLE

This is an excellent cold remedy and a charming warm-weather drink served with ice.

4 cups water
2 cups lemon juice, freshly squeezed
2 tablespoons fresh lavender flowers and leaves
    (use L. intermedia var. 'Grosso')
3 cups sugar
6 cloves
4 or 5 strips lemon zest

Simmer everything together in a closed saucepan for 10 minutes. Set aside to cool overnight. Strain the next morning. Serve with iced water for a cooling drink or add a dash of brandy to ½ cup of lavender syrup topped up with boiling water as a winter warmer.

LAVENDER TEAS AND DRINKS

Once you realise what a wonderfully relaxing and calming herb lavender is, you will want to include it in your daily menu, especially because we are all so over-stressed and anxious and even little children nowadays are put under enormous strain to keep up with all that is happening around them. One distraught mother of two sons said: 'Whatever happened to a happy childhood?' These young boys are battling to 'perform' in school, sport, in their peer group and even in the holidays, which are now crammed with extra maths and extra computer classes – where will it all end?

So I put together this refreshing collection of unwinding recipes to help you de-stress. And they taste delicious! And they are good for you!

LAVENDER, MELISSA AND GRENADILLA UNWINDER

SERVES 6

This is a delicious tea for children to take to school in their juice bottles, so keep a jug in the fridge. Grenadilla has calming, unwinding and relaxing qualities.

1 litre boiling water
½ cup fresh lavender flowers (L. intermedia var. 'Margaret Roberts')
½ cup melissa sprigs
1 cinnamon stick
1 litre grenadilla unsweetened juice

Pour the boiling water over the lavender flowers, melissa sprigs and cinnamon stick. Let it stand until it cools, about 2 hours. Strain. Add the grenadilla juice. Mix with the strained tea and sweeten with a touch of honey if liked. Chill. Serve with ice.

LAVENDER AFTER DINNER COFFEE

Lavender and coffee combine deliciously. As an end to a meal, infuse a thumb length of lavender flowers in your favourite black filter coffee and sweeeten with a touch of lavender flavoured sugar, or gently stir with a lavender sprig to get the flavour.

Lavender coffee

LAVENDER PUNCH

SERVES 10

This is a party favourite and the drink that I serve at Christmas dinner and all celebrations.

20 allspice berries (pimento)
20 cardamom pods
2 litres boiling water
6 stalks lavender flowers (L. intermedia var. 'Margaret Roberts'), enough to fill 1 cup lightly packed
zest of 1 lemon
juice of 1 lemon
1 litre fresh pineapple juice
1 litre fresh grenadilla juice
pulp of 10 grenadillas
a few slices of fresh pineapple, thinly sliced into little fan shapes
a little sugar

Crush the allspice berries and the cardamom pods lightly to release their flavour. Pour boiling water over the allspice berries, cardamom pods and lavender stalks. Add the zest and juice of the lemon. Let everything stand till cool, about 2 hours. Strain. Add the pineapple juice and the grenadilla juice. Add the grenadilla pulp and several slices of fresh pineapple. Sweeten with a little sugar if necessary. Serve chilled in a big glass bowl.

COOK'S TIP

I pack ice all around the punch bowl and float rose petals, little lavender sprigs, violets and slices of lemon in the bowl. I also tuck maidenhair fern, rosebuds and gardenias into the ice – all are edible and it makes the big punch bowl look so pretty and festive.

LAVENDER DE-STRESS HOT TEA

SERVES 1

This is my quick-fix tea when it all gets to be too much!

1 cup boiling water
¼ cup fresh lavender flowers (L. intermedia var. 'Margaret Roberts')
thumb-size piece of cinnamon
1 teaspoon honey

Pour the boiling water over the lavender flowers and cinnamon. Add the honey, and let stand for 5 minutes, then strain. Sip slowly.

LAVENDER AND BERRY TEA

SERVES 6

This has become one of our best-selling teas in the Herbal Centre tea garden. Visitors love its refreshing taste and we make great urns of it for our open days. It is delicious and can also be served chilled, in a tall glass.

In a teapot pour 1 litre boiling water over ½ cup lavender flowers (L. intermedia var. 'Margaret Roberts')
2 tea bags berry tea (bought at the supermarket)
2 teaspoons lemon zest
1 tablespoon honey

Let stand about 5 minutes, then pour into cups and add more boiling water to the pot – there's lots of flavour for a second cup.

COOK'S TIP

When we have strawberries and raspberries in season, we make a syrup with the berries and sugar, equal quantities, in a little water and add some of the syrup to the teapot.

LAVENDER ANTI-CHILL DRINK

SERVES 1

For a winter evening after a frantic day this warming drink takes some beating.

1 cup boiling water
1 thumb-length sprig of lavender (L. intermedia var. 'Margaret Roberts')
1 star anise
1 slice lemon
a little lemon juice
2 teaspoons grated ginger
1-2 teaspoons honey
a little dash of brandy

Pour the boiling water over all the other ingredients. Let stand for 3-5 minutes, then strain. Sip slowly and feel the tension melt away.

COOK'S TIP

If you feel that you are starting a cold or flu and your throat is sore, add ¼ cup fresh sage leaves and an extra slice of lemon to the above recipe.

LAVENDER AND ROSE PETAL TEA

SERVES 1

This is a beautiful tea to sip while you relax in a lavender-scented bath. I call it my 'pampering tea' when I've been too rushed, too tired and too strung out. It literally irons away the tension.

1 cup boiling water
1 thumb-length piece of lavender (L. intermedia var. 'Margaret Roberts')
¼ cup fresh unsprayed rose petals (my favourite is Crimson Glory)
4 cardamom pods, lightly crushed
1 teaspoon honey (optional)
1 vanilla pod to stir (optional)

Pour boiling water over all the other ingredients. Let stand for 3-5 minutes, then strain. Add a teaspoon of honey if you like and if you have it, stir with a vanilla pod. Relax and sip slowly.

LAVENDER MILK SHAKE

SERVES 1

This was one of my children's favourite treats, and it is a healthy virtually unsweetened alternative to the normal milk shake. Make one at a time in a liquidiser.

1 glass milk

1 banana

½ cup sultanas that have been soaked in a little hot
    water for about 10 minutes

1 teaspoon lavender flowers, stripped off their
    stems (L. intermedia var. 'Margaret Roberts'
    or 'Grosso')

½ teaspoon cinnamon powder

½ teaspoon ground nutmeg, grated freshly into the
    drink from a whole nutmeg

2 tablespoons plain yoghurt

Discard the water in which the sultanas have been soaked. Whirl all the ingredients together in a liquidiser for 3 minutes. Pour the frothy drink into a tall glass and enjoy it! It's good for you!

LAVENDER HONEY AND MILK
BEDTIME DRINK

SERVES 1

For a calming nightcap warm a cup of milk with a sprig of lavender in it (use L. intermedia var. 'Margaret Roberts' or 'Grosso') for about 4 minutes –

do not let it boil. Remove the lavender sprig. Sweeten with a touch of lavender honey and sip slowly. Sweet dreams!

LAVENDER ICE DRINK

SERVES 1

When the day has been too hot and you are too weary and too frazzled this is a little lifesaver.

In a tall glass pack in about 1 cup of crushed ice, pour over this 2 teaspoons of apple cider vinegar and a dash of lavender syrup (see page 111) and top up with cold water. Stir vigorously. Relax for 10 minutes and sip slowly.

COOK'S TIP

Apple cider vinegar is an exceptional ingredient to keep in the kitchen cupboard. Its effects are nothing short of amazing and here in this deliciously cooling drink it literally removes acid build-up that the day has brought and so releases the tension. Combined with lavender's calming and unwinding properties this is a match made in heaven.

If you don't have the lavender syrup on hand, warm 2 sprigs of lavender flowers in ½ cup honey for 5 minutes, strain out the lavender and add a teaspoon or two to the iced water you pour over the crushed ice.

Lavender in cosmetics

Warning: For sensitive skins, always test a little of any recipe on the inside of the wrist first. Leave on for 10 minutes to see if there is any reaction.

Lavender has been used since the earliest centuries to heal, soothe and beautify the skin. The early Greeks and Romans were particularly fond of lavender and used it as a strewing herb on the floors of the bathhouses and parlours, and in their washing waters.

One of the earliest ways of using lavender was as a scrub. Fresh sprigs and flowers were used, tied in linen squares and soaked in hot water, often with soapwort (Sapponaria officinalis) to give soapiness, and the lavender they used was either L. angustifolia, or L. stoechas, the Spanish lavender. Students in our classes have experimented with these combinations and they used equal quantities of lavender and soapwort tied in a square of cotton and they find if it is well soaked under the hot water tap, it makes a marvellous bath bag.

There are recipes that go back into the sixteenth century where lard soap was grated or finely chopped, fresh lavender leaves were added and tied into a 'kerchief' as they called it. The bag was used to scrub the entire body. We have experimented with all the lavenders and find these the best: Lavandula stoechas *group or Spanish lavenders, the* L. *intermedia var.* 'Margaret Roberts' *and* 'Grosso', *and* L. *latifolia* 'Grandmother's lavender'. *They give the strongest oils and help to unwind and relax the whole body.*

LAVENDER SOAPS, SOAKS AND SCRUBS

Our grandmothers used lavender water as a wash for oily coarse skin. It was simply made by boiling 1 cup of lavender leaves and flowers in 4 cups of water for 10 minutes and then letting it cool. Strained and kept in the fridge, this was used with pads of cotton wool soaked in it, or as a wash.

Through the years I have found this simple treatment to be excellent – not only for oily problem skin, but as an astringent – as lavender contain tannins – a freshener, a toner and, in a spritz bottle a wonderful summer cooler, sprayed over face, neck and arms. Perfect for travelling! Is it not time that we go back into these wonderful old recipes and make them for their pure simplicity and pleasure?

LAVENDER BATH SOAP

Lavender bath soap makes a lovely gift – even lovelier to spoil yourself. This is quickly and easily made and is excellent for oily, problem skin.

Lavender bath soap

2-3 cakes plain baby soap or any plain soap (to make 4 cups)
1 cup chopped lavender leaves and flowers (L. intermedia var. 'Margaret Roberts' or 'Grosso')
1 cup boiling water
3 tablespoons lavender flowers and buds, stripped from their stems
1 teaspoon lavender essential oil (optional)
1-3 drops mauve food colouring

Line several small dishes with plastic wrap to make moulds. Grate the soap into a saucepan. Place the chopped lavender leaves and flowers in the water and boil for 10 minutes. Cool for 10 minutes, then strain. Add to the grated soap and boil gently for 5 minutes, stirring all the time. Stir in the lavender flowers and buds stripped from their stems, the lavender essential oil (optional) and the mauve food colouring. Stir well. Pour the mixture into moulds. Leave to set. Once set, pull off the plastic wrap, and with a sharp knife trim any rough edges. Wrap in greaseproof paper and store for 1 month before using.

LAVENDER BATH

A lavender bath is the perfect panacea for aching muscles, sore feet and legs, aching back and shoulders, stress and anxiety and a problem skin. It will soothe away tension and help you to relax and unwind. To really pamper yourself light a lavender-scented candle, play some gentle, quiet, relaxing music, take a few deep breaths and ... relax in the warm scented water. You will emerge feeling wonderful and you will sleep like a baby.

4 cups lavender sprigs, leaves and flowers (L. latifolia, L. allardii 'African Pride')
3 litres water
6 drops pure lavender essential oil

Simmer the lavender sprigs, leaves and flowers in the water for 20 minutes. Strain and add to your bath-water. Just before you get into the bath add six drops only of pure lavender essential oil to the bath-water.

LAVENDER FOOT BATH

A lavender foot bath is deodorising, refreshing and wonderful after a hard day on your feet. It can be very helpful to elderly people in assisting them to regulate their sleep pattern, as well as for aches and pains.

sprigs of freshly picked lavender leaves (L. allardii and L. allardi 'African Pride')
2 kettles boiling water
1 cup Epsom salts
lavender cream (see recipe on page 118)

Place a large shallow basin on the floor in front of a comfortable chair. Pack in the sprigs of lavender leaves. Pour water over this. Leave to draw and cool until pleasantly warm. Mix in the Epsom salts, and sit with feet immersed, resting on the lavender sprigs for 10-15 minutes. Wriggle your toes, rub your feet with the lavender sprigs and relax. Briskly towel-dry and massage in some lavender cream. Put on cotton socks.

LAVENDER BATH BAG

This is our modern-day version of the bath bag. It is good for soothing away stress, anxiety and fatigue.

2 cups fresh lavender leaves and flowers

Pack the lavender leaves and flowers into a handkerchief, or a square of fine fabric or into a quickly-made drawstring bag (soft pure cotton). Soak in a hot bath and use the bag or bundle of tied-up lavender as a sponge. I use it with soap rubbed onto it as a fragrant scrub. Once the bath is over, discard the lavender leaves and flowers, rinse out the bag and dry. Use fresh lavender for every bath.

LAVENDER AND OATMEAL SCRUB

My grandmother's lavender, Lavandula latifolia, *and* L. allardii *'African Pride' are superb for this lavender and oatmeal scrub. Monks in the Middle Ages used the stoechas lavender leaves. Experiment with them all. I love using this scrub after air travel – it seems to ease jet lag.*

2 cups boiling water
2 cups fresh lavender leaves, stripped off their stems
2 cups oatmeal
1 cup plain yoghurt

In a large saucepan pour the water over the lavender leaves. Leave to draw for 10 minutes. Add the oats (I use the big flake non-instant kind), mix in well, and press down in the hot lavender water. Heat gently for 5 minutes, then cool to a comfortable temperature. Add the yoghurt and mix well. Stand in the bath and, taking handfuls at a time, rub briskly and spread all over your body. It will be messy, but it is marvellous for sloughing off dead cells and revitalising sluggish dull skin. Lie back in the bath and relax. You'll emerge feeling wonderfully glowing and relaxed.

NOTE: *Place a plug strainer over the bath plug to prevent your drains from becoming clogged. These strainers are readily available from hardware stores.*

LAVENDER BODY LOTIONS AND CREAMS

SUMMER LAVENDER BODY LOTION

This is my favourite body lotion. In winter I add more moisturising oils.

1 cup good aqueous cream
1 cup fresh lavender flowers, stripped off their stems
(L. intermedia var. 'Margaret Roberts' or Grandmother's lavender, L. latifolia)
1½ cups distilled water
3 teaspoons vitamin E oil
1 teaspoon pure lavender essential oil
2 tablespoons almond oil

Simmer the aqueous cream and the lavender flowers together in a double boiler for 20 minutes, then strain. Spoon the aqueous cream and lavender mixture into a liquidiser. Add the distilled water, vitamin E oil, pure lavender essential oil and almond oil. Whirl the ingredients for 2 minutes in the liquidiser, or whisk with an egg whisk. Spoon into a sterilised jar or bottle and seal well. Use lavishly, especially on your legs and feet.

WARNING

Test a little on the inside of your wrist to see if it is gentle enough for your skin. If there is any redness leave out the lavender essential oil.

WINTER LAVENDER BODY LOTION

Use the recipe for summer lavender body lotion, but add:

1-2 tablespoons flax-seed oil
2 tablespoons grape-seed oil

Add these additional ingredients to the liquidiser, and at the end whirl for an extra 2 minutes. These two ingredients will make the lotion very rich and beautifully moisturising and soothing for dry winter skin.

LAVENDER NOURISHING CREAM

This lavender nourishing cream is lovely for winter use and for cracked heels and rough skin all year round.

1 cup aqueous cream
½ cup almond oil
1 cup lavender leaves and flowers (L. intermedia var. 'Margaret Roberts')
2 teaspoons wheatgerm oil
2 teaspoons grape-seed oil

Warm the aqueous cream, almond oil and the lavender leaves and flowers in a double boiler. Simmer for 20 minutes, stirring occasionally. Strain and add the wheatgerm oil and grape-seed oil. Mix well. Pour into a sterilised screw-top jar. Apply lavishly!

LAVENDER FACE AND BODY TREATMENTS

LAVENDER AND CUCUMBER MASK

The astringent qualities of lavender combine beautifully here with the soothing, deeply cleansing action of the cucumber. This mask is simple and quick to make. I use it frequently during the hot months after a heavy day in my office. The ancient Greeks used this recipe with plain yoghurt. The yoghurt acts as a cleanser and has anti-acid properties, so it makes a superb skin treatment.

1 cup cucumber pieces
1 cup lavender leaves (use L. stoechas here)
½ cup plain yoghurt (optional)

Mash up cucumber and lavender in a food processor and add the yoghurt if you want to include it in the mash. Lie back in a hot bath and pack the mixture over your face and neck. Leave on for 10 minutes. Rinse off with warm water.

LAVENDER CELLULITE OIL

This can be used as an all-over massage oil for loosening cellulite. It is also wonderful for tired shoulders and upper arms. The oil is best applied just before a bath so that it can continue its work with the hot water as you lie back and soak.

1 cup almond oil
½ cup chopped lavender leaves and flowers (L. intermedia var. 'Margaret Roberts' or 'Grosso')
6 cloves, lightly crushed
1 tablespoon rosewater
2 teaspoons wheatgerm oil
½ teaspoon lavender essential oil

Warm everything together in a double boiler for 20 minutes with the lid on. Stir well every now and then. Strain. Cool. Add the lavender essential oil. Pour into a screw-top bottle. Massage into the thighs using circular movements. Stand the bottle in a jug of hot water to warm oil before use.

LAVENDER HAIR-CARE

LAVENDER HAIR RINSE

This lavender hair rinse is excellent for oily hair, as well as for scalp itchiness and dryness. Deeply cleansing, it can occasionally replace a conditioner. Do not underestimate the importance of this rinse; it is a true toner and will clear all sorts of scalp problems.

2 cups fresh lavender leaves and flowers (L. intermedia var. 'Margaret Roberts')
3 litres water
½ cup apple cider vinegar

Boil the lavender leaves and flowers in 2 litres water for 10 minutes. Leave to stand and cool until pleasantly warm. Strain and add the apple cider vinegar and 1 litre warm water. Pour into the basin and use as a final rinse after shampooing hair. Massage well into scalp.

LAVENDER FRAGRANCES

BASIC LAVENDER PERFUME

When I was studying aromatherapy and plant fragrances, our charming French lecturer always stressed the use of fewer rather than more scented ingredients in making up fragrant oils and perfumes. She urged us not to 'confuse the nose'. So this is how we began, and I am still experimenting twenty-five years on. I find this a fascinating hobby.

2 cups fresh lavender flowers, stripped off their stems (the best here is Lavandula intermedia *var. 'Grosso')*
1 cup vodka or cane spirit
10 cloves
¼ cup cinnamon pieces

Pour everything into a large glass jar with a screw-top lid and shake well. Leave in a dark cupboard for 3 weeks so that the fragrance can mature.

Shake up daily, morning and evening, a minute at a time. Strain and discard the lavender and the spices. Repeat with fresh lavender and spices until you get the perfume that you desire. I did the procedure 10 times, long ago, and achieved a wonderfully rich lavender fragrance and it still remains fragrant today, but you can short cut this by adding 20 drops of lavender essential oil to the strained mixture. Ensure that you keep it well sealed at all times. I use this not only as a refreshing perfume spray, but also in a spritz bottle, as a linen and room spray. Shake the bottle frequently to disperse the essential oil.

HINT

I find that L. intermedia var. 'Grosso' and L. latifolia are best for making basic lavender perfume. You could combine these two lavenders if you like the scent. Or you could use jasmine flowers, carnation petals, lemon verbena leaves or rose petals, depending on your preference. But remember to use a singular flower scent 'so as not to confuse the nose'!

Some of the Woolworths Margaret Roberts Collection of the lavender core range that has proved to be eternally popular!

Lavender 'eau-de-Cologne'

This is the way the famous eau-de-Cologne was developed originally and it is great fun to try it for your own use.

¾ cup lemon, rind very well dried
½ cup orange rind very well dried
2½ cups vodka (or brandy as was used in ancient days)
1 full cup of fresh lavender flowers, stripped off their stems (Choose your favourite. I use L. latifolia *or* L. intermedia *var. 'Margaret Roberts' or 'Grosso' or* L. angustifolia *var. 'Hidcote' – if I'm lucky to find flowers – or* L. allardii.)
½ cup fresh bergamot leaves
½ cup fresh rosemary leaves, stripped off the stems
20 cloves
2 sticks of cinnamon (about ¼ cup of cinnamon bark)

Use a potato peeler to thinly pare away the bright yellow rind from fresh well-washed lemons with no pith. Dry the pieces in the sun on a tray. Turn often. Dry the orange rind in the same way. Mix the lavender flowers, bergamot leaves and the rosemary leaves together with the rinds. Press the herb-and-peel mixture into a large glass jar with a good screw top. Add 20 cloves and 2 sticks of cinnamon. Pour in the vodka and shake well. Place in a dark cupboard and shake up for 2 minutes every day, twice a day – morning and evening – for three weeks. Strain, carefully pressing out every drop. Discard mixture of herbs, spices and peel, and if you like the smell start enjoying it. I use it in a spritz bottle to refresh, and as a room spray.

If the scent is not strong enough, repeat the procedure using the same vodka that you strained out. Always store in a cool dark place. Use up within three months as the scent evaporates.

Lavender splash-on deodorant

This is the deodorant that our grandmothers used. It is refreshing, cooling and pure natural goodness.

1 cup fresh lavender flowers (use Grandmother's lavender, Lavandula latifolia *or Dutch lavender,* L. allardii)
1½ cups apple cider vinegar
½ cup cloves
½ cup star anise
½ cup fresh rosemary sprigs
½ cup fresh sage leaves
2 fresh-flowering lavender stems (as above)

Simmer gently together in a small heavy-bottomed pot for 10 minutes, stirring occasionally. Cover and leave to stand until cool. Strain and discard herbs, cloves and star anise. Pour into a screw-top jar and add lavender stems for quick identification.

To use

Wash under arms thoroughly. Dry with a fluffy towel. Mix 1 tablespoon deodorant with 2 tablespoons water. Use a cottonwool pad or splash on under arms.

Lavender in aromatherapy

Helen Keller, who was blind and deaf from birth, wrote: 'Smell is a potent wizard that transports us across thousands of miles and all the years we have lived. Odours, instantaneous and fleeting, cause the heart to dilate joyously, or contract with remembered grief.'

Perhaps this is why the scent of lavender will forever remain so loved – it is part of childhood and memories, and woven into our lives. My youngest child, my daughter Sandra, was eleven years old when I took my first tour to the herb gardens of England, which included the breathtaking Norfolk Lavender fields – the highlight of the trip. I was away a month and she sent me little 'homesick' notes, and I realised it had been a difficult time for my whole family while I had been away. On opening my suitcase the moment I returned, the room was flooded with the scent of lavender which I'd brought from Norfolk, and it engulfed my tearful little girl. From that day to this she is transported back to the time I was away, and can hardly bear the smell of the English lavenders!

We have grown in the Herbal Centre gardens both Lavandula angustifolia *var. 'Hidcote', and the new* L. angustifolia *var. 'Swampy', both with that typical English lavender scent, and I often pick little bunches for her to try to lift the feeling of homesick heartache from over twenty years ago, and she still tearfully, laughingly, flees from it.*

The power of scent is compelling, and I close my eyes every now and then while I'm working with my Grandmother's lavender, and I am transported to her little cottage in Gordon's Bay, and I can hear the sound of the sea and the South Easter howling around the house, as the scent engulfs me, and I hear her voice and feel the warmth of the fire as we tossed the little bundles of stripped lavender sticks onto it, and I am eight years old again.

Lavender essential oil does that memory-making trick exceptionally well, and the art is to find a quiet place and a quiet moment to treat yourself either with a massage oil, or on a candle or burner, or in the bath, and to relax and unwind, not with fear or anxiety or stress or anguish as companions, but just as a moment of unwinding, so that you never associate the preciousness of lavender with those negative feelings.

We know that lavender is calming, soothing, unwinding, relaxing and de-stressing; we know that it will give us the quietness we so sorely seek. So go for a walk or a jog, or do a bit of exercise or gardening before you give yourself that lavender treatment, so as not to lock into your brain and body any of those anxious feelings, and you won't cry like Sandy does when she smells the evocative scent of English lavender!

In its present revival, the art of aromatherapy seems very much a part of today's living, a soothing antidote against stress, exhaustion, burnout and anxiety, and its close companion, tension. But how astonishing to realise that ancient Greek, Roman and Egyptian writings make frequent reference to lavender's therapeutic and beautifying properties.

They, the ancient medicine men, classified lavender as calming, soothing, tonic and sedative. In the twelfth and thirteenth centuries it was used to treat colds and coughs, plagues, poor circulation, heart and liver ailments as well as apoplexy and epileptic and mental derangements. What is fascinating is that the oils of the *L. intermedias*, *L. latifolias* and the *stoechas* lavenders have similar properties to the *L. angustifolias*, which is the usual lavender oil on the market. So try all of them.

Today the pure distilled essential oil of lavender is still being used to treat these ailments – antiseptic, antispasmodic, are perhaps extra names added to its royal list, but ever more so, lavender oil finds its place on many a bathroom shelf to apply neat to bites, stings, burns, to add a drop or two to a bath for a hyperactive child, or a distraught teenager and her equally upset mother, and generally to be used as a panacea for everything from a 'flu epidemic to nausea, headaches to gout, menopause to shingles! And it smells glorious!

THE AROMATIC OILS

Aromatherapy is expanding into new essential oils, which is exciting and inspiring. Remember that when you buy true lavender oil from England, France and Italy, it is inevitably the typical *Lavandula angustifolia*. This is the lavender oil on which the world market is based. But new oils are constantly emerging. Our own Southern Hemisphere lavenders like the *intermedias*, *allardiis* and *latifolias* offer superb oils.

More exciting than anything is distilling your own oil. Imagine getting a few drops of pure lavender oil from a couple of large bunches of your own organically grown lavender that you pick and process immediately. Not only is the process fascinating, but the thrill of using your own oil is tangible.

Lavender oil has a well-established tradition behind it. It is one of the world's most popular oils. There are mainly three types of lavender oils on the world market at present: true lavender oil, lavandin and spike lavender. Although *L. stoechas* is not among these, it is still being extracted in Spain to a small extent, the way it was centuries ago.

Like fashion, the popularity of the various lavender oils waxes and wanes in different countries. What remains steadfast is that lavender oil has always topped the list of favourite essential oils on the world market.

TRUE LAVENDER OIL

This is the basic essential lavender oil for Europe. Its constituents occur in the ratio and amount that the market looks for. This lavender is grown mainly in France, and to a lesser degree in parts of Italy and England. Note that these countries are all in the Northern Hemisphere.

Synonyms *Lavandula officinalis*, *L. angustifolia*, English lavender, Lavender Vera

Safety data Non-toxic, non-irritant, non-sensitising

Extraction The essential oil is extracted by steam distillation from the fresh-flowering tops. Steam distillation is the most economical way of extracting the oil. The emerging oil is virtually colourless. It has a 'floral herbaceous' scent with a balsamic woody undertone. This exquisite oil blends particularly well with citrus, cedarwood, clove, clary sage, rose geranium, oak moss, patchouli, pine and vetiver oils.

An 'absolute' and a 'concrete' are produced by a solvent extraction in smaller quantities. This oil is a dark green, sticky, viscous liquid with a very sweet herbaceous and lightly floral scent. It is used mainly by the perfume industry.

Principal constituents This vital analysis indicates the most sought after constituents, and all the oils differ. It must be a fascinating exercise for the biochemists and scientists analysing the quantities of these constituents. There are over 100 constituents in this true lavender. Here are a few of them, to give you an idea of what the

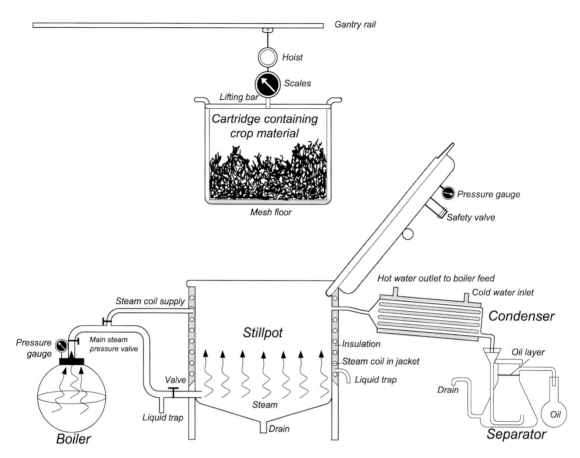

The distilling process is simplified and is not to scale here, but this will give a good idea of how to build a still.
SOURCE: *Lavender: a grower's guide,* by JA McGimpsey & NG Potter. A New Zealand Crop Research Publication.

market requires in greater or lesser quantities, to give that literally breathtaking marketable oil.

Lavender comprises up to 40 per cent linalyl acetate. The other major constituents exist in varying quantities depending on where they are grown. Altitude, weather, soil, and time of harvesting influence the composition of these constituents.

Note that the true lavenders are all Northern Hemisphere lavenders.

Linalol, lavandulol, lavandulyl acetate, terpineol, cineol, ocimene, linalool, caryophyllene, limonene, camphor and borneol are among the other constituents. These are often the constituents by which a lavender oil is judged and which make the fragrance famous.

A trained 'nose' is exceptionally valuable in the 'aromatic' industry. He/she can tell whether an oil or, for that matter, a perfume will be popular or not. In the armomatherapy oils we know that if it smells good the client will respond well. This is why lavender is so appealing – it smells wonderful.

ACTIONS OF TRUE LAVENDER ESSENTIAL OIL
When you look at this list of healing properties you will understand why lavender oil is so popular: analgesic, anticonvulsive, antidepressant, antiseptic, anti-spasmodic, antirheumatic, carminative, meaning able to expel wind, cholaqoque meaning that which benefits

the liver, diuretic, emmenagogue which means the power to promote menstruation, hypotensive, nervine, rubefacient, sedative, tonic, vermifuge.

USES

Skin care To treat abscesses, acne, athlete's foot, boils, bruises, burns, dandruff, earache, inflammation, insect bites and stings, insect repellent, lice, ringworm, skin sores, scabies, spots, sunburn, cuts, grazes, wounds.

Circulation, muscles and joints In a massage cream or oil for backache, sciatica, strains, sprains, rheumatic aches and pains, cold tired sore feet.

Respiratory system For asthma, bronchitis, catarrh, halitosis, laryngitis, coughs, 'flu, whooping cough, sore throat.

In steam Dissolve a few drops in boiling water, make a towel tent over your head and inhale the vapour. Or use in a carrier oil over throat and chest – ratio usually 1 drop in 10–20 drops carrier oil.

In a massage oil Used to relieve headaches, depression, hypertension, insomnia, migraine, nervous tension, anxiety, cramps, fear, stress-related conditions, PMS, shock, vertigo, colic, cystitis, indigestion and nausea.

Other uses True lavender oil is used in pharmaceutical, antiseptic and antibacterial ointments, soaps, lotions and perfumes.

LAVANDIN

Lavandin is a *Lavandula intermedia* essential oil. Although this is a lavender oil, it is commonly known on the world market as 'lavandin'. It is becoming increasingly popular.

Synonyms *Lavandin*, *Lavandula intermedia*, Sterile lavender, *Lavandula hybrida*

Safety data Non-toxic, non-irritant, non-sensitising

Extraction Lavandins are extracted from the fresh-flowering tops of any of the *intermedias*, but never mix a variety. Always use one singular lavender. A lot of this information is based on *L. intermedia* var. 'Grosso', but the other *intermedias* including our own *L. intermedia* var. 'Margaret Roberts' show the same constituents and uses.

An almost colourless or pale yellow oil is obtained by steam distillation, which has a fresh camphoraceous top note. In a good-quality oil the camphoraceous note should not be too high, and its undertone is woody herbaceous, which fits in perfectly. These pleasant notes blend well with other wood-like oils: clove, bay, cinnamon, cypress, pine, nutmeg, sage, rose geranium, clary sage, thyme, rosemary, lemon, lime and the beautiful bergamot orange oil. Some essential oil growers combine lavandin, lime, patchouli, sage and thyme oils with a touch of cinnamon as an extraordinary insect repelling oil that can be diluted in a good carrier oil and rubbed onto the skin.

An absolute and a concrete are produced by a solvent extraction and this is thick, dark greenish brown, and is more richly oak moss and camphorous. It is used in the cosmetic and perfume industry. *Lavandula intermedia* var. 'Grosso' gives a superb absolute that is becoming very popular in the perfume industry, and it is sometimes partnered with patchouli absolute for particularly men's cosmetics like aftershave and shampoos. It is a strong fresh deodorising herbaceous scent that smells good.

Principal constituents Linalyl acetate is the most abundant constituent, 30–34 per cent. The next highest is linalool cineol, and pinene and camphene are quite strong. There are also traces of borneol and lavandulol with lavandulyl acetate. In New Zealand the other important lavandin cultivars differ slightly, but overall give the results that make the oils so fabulous. They use 'Grosso', 'Super', 'Impress Purple', 'Bogong', 'Old English' – which is very similar to *L. intermedia* var. 'Margaret Roberts' – and 'Grey Hedge' – which we have trialled and found does not flower reliably, and which is very high in cineole and limonene.

The tables on page 126 will give you an idea of the differences, for interest.

ACTIONS OF LAVANDIN ESSENTIAL OIL

Lavandula intermedia var. 'Grosso' particularly gives a similar action to *Lavandula angustifolia*. It too, like the *angustifolias*, has antiseptic, antifungal, antispasmodic,

Analysis of essential oils from different L. angustifolia and Lavandin cultivars grown at Redbank Research Station, Clyde, New Zealand

L. angustifolia cultivars and selections						
Component	Munstead (Clyde)	Munstead (Omarama)	Munstead 5/14	L. angustifolia (Tarras)	L. angustifolia (Christchurch)	Twickel Purple
1,8 Cincole + Limonene	1.63	2.70	0.49	0.00	2.66	0.97
trans-β-Ocimene	0.48	0.53	2.35	2.06	0.55	0.52
cis-β-Ocimene	4.51	5.84	7.85	7.12	5.52	6.13
Camphor	0.00	0.00	0.00	0.00	0.00	0.00
Linalool	24.12	25.06	31.46	41.80	25.30	24.60
Linalyl acetate	49.93	43.55	15.14	23.33	43.41	40.90
Terpinen-1 ol-4	7.13	8.08	18.93	0.00	8.13	4.91
Borneol + Lavandulol	0.00	0.00	0.00	0.00	0.00	0.00
Lavandulyl acetate	0.00	1.56	3.09	2.96	1.55	1.55

Lavandin cultivars						
Component	Grosso	Super	Impress Purple	Bogong	Old English	Grey Hedge
1,8 Cincole + Limonene	3.46	5.94	4.10	5.12	8.81	12.54
trans-β-Ocimene	0.35	0.91	0.47	0.29	2.35	2.01
cis-β-Ocimene	2.21	4.04	2.34	2.40	6.55	8.67
Camphor	5.56	6.54	5.44	8.60	0.00	6.23
Linalool	26.90	36.38	25.86	42.09	42.34	37.22
Linalyl acetate	40.42	30.31	39.88	19.44	7.97	7.91
Terpinen-1 ol-4	1.54	0.00	1.19	0.52	3.82	2.78
Borneol + Lavandulol	2.40	2.23	2.73	5.43	9.38	3.93
Lavandulyl acetate	2.22	0.97	2.03	0.30	0.98	0.92

SOURCE: *Lavender: a grower's guide*, by JA McGimpsey & NG Potter. A New Zealand Crop Research Publication.

analgesic and antirheumatic properties and is also superb for treating tension, anxiety, fear, depression and panic. It will also expel wind, act as a diuretic and lower the heart rate and eases muscular spasm and often even night sweats and nervous tension. It is an infinitely comforting oil.

USES

The lavandins are excellent in skin care; hair care; and in creams to soothe aching muscles, athlete's foot, rashes, grazes and sunburn. Like true lavender oil it can be used in soaps, detergents, antibacterial ointments, perfumes and soothing gels and lotions.

Used as an inhalant – drops of the oil in a big basin of boiling water and a towel over the head – the lavandin fragrance gets to the very source of a blocked nose, blocked sinuses, bronchitis and congested lungs, and a few drops – no more than 4 or 5 – in the bath are infinitely comforting when you're aching with 'flu.

All the *intermedias* have similar actions to true lavender and 'Grosso', 'Super' and 'Impress Purple' have the best fragrance, closest to *Lavandula angustifolia*, so it is worth really studying these four for oil production. They all do well in the Southern African climate, especially 'Grosso' and 'Super'.

SPIKE LAVENDER

This old-fashioned lavender oil, high in camphorenes, is the oil from 'Grandmother's lavender'. Powerful and potent, this was one of the first lavenders to be used in oil production around the eleventh and twelfth centuries. In the sixteenth century there was a popular preparation 'oleum spicae' made by the monks, and later the 'apothecers', who were the first chemists. This preparation, which was intended as a remedy for paralysed limbs, stiff sore arthritic joints and sprains, was made by mixing turpentine with oil of spike, half and half.

Synonyms Lavandula latifolia, Grandmother's lavender, oil of spike.

Safety data Use this oil only in a carrier oil as it can cause irritation to the skin, and sensitivity on the skin in pure form. The safest is in the ratio 1 in 20 (i.e. 1 teaspoon of pure oil of spike in 20 teaspoons carrier oil, for example almond oil).

Extraction The essential oil is extracted only by water or steam distillation from the flowering tops. A pure colourless, or, in rare cases, the palest yellow oil emerges with a penetrating and strong fresh herbaceous and camphoraceous odour. Of all the lavender oils this has the strongest scent, and is the most potent.

Because the oil is so strong it is a stand-alone oil, but it can be combined with other strong essential oils like sage, eucalyptus, pine, cedar wood, clove, nutmeg and patchouli oils.

Principal constituents Oil of spike is mainly rich in cineol and camphor – 40% to 60% – but it has smaller quantities of linalool and linalyl. This is what gives the strong and powerful scent that was used in the early centuries to revive people from fainting fits.

ACTIONS OF OIL OF SPIKE

It is important to remember that this is the most powerful of all the lavender oils. Oil of spike has analgesic, anticonvulsive, antifungal, antibacterial, antiseptic, antispasmodic and antirheumatic qualities. It is also an active diuretic with superb de-stress, antidepressant and hypotensive actions. Oil of spike can be used to treat nervousness, anxiety, burn-out and extreme tension.

USES

The skin Use for all sorts of skin infections, including athlete's foot, boils, sores, bruises, burns, earache (massaged behind the ears), insect bites and stings, an effective insect repellent, and for scabies, ringworm, cuts, grazes, sunburn but *always in a carrier oil*.

Circulation, joints and muscles In a massage cream or carrier oil, it is superb for backache and sciatica, aching stiff shoulders, neck and legs, strains, sprains and aching feet.

Respiratory system Inhaling the steam of drops of oil of spike in hot water with a towel tent over the head will ease asthma, blocked sinuses, stuffy nose, catarrh, sinus headache, 'flu and cold symptoms.

Massage oil For all the above symptoms, oil of spike with a good carrier oil is astonishing in its effectiveness. But always use with caution and always test on the inside of the wrist first.

Other uses Oil of spike is used extensively in pharmaceutical preparations, especially in veterinary practice as a prophylactic, for incipient paralysis, for arthritis, rheumatism, and to get rid of fleas and lice.

Oil of spike is an important component in disinfectants, industrial deodorisers and cleaning agents, insecticides and room sprays, as antibacterial and antiviral, and in varnishes and lacquers for preserving wood.

As far as I can ascertain, oil of spike is not yet produced in the Southern Hemisphere. When you realise all its power, shouldn't this be a crop for commercial growers? Perhaps this will be one of the important oils for South Africa in the future. Wouldn't my grandmother be proud?

PATCH TEST

Remember, essential oils are powerful, potent and concentrated. ***Always*** patch test essential oils as they can burn the skin.

Dilute in a carrier oil like almond oil, grape-seed oil, or even medicinal olive oil. You can buy these carrier oils at your local pharamacy.

Start with the 1% dilution, which is 1 drop of your lavender essential oil in 1 teaspoon of carrier oil. Stir well and apply a little onto the inner wrist or on the inside of the elbow. Massage in lightly and leave on as long as possible – aromatherapists say for 12 hours. If there is any adverse reaction – reddening or itching – rub on a little pure almond oil, then wash off immediately with a second wash to make sure that it is all gone. If there is any redness I squeeze over it the fresh juice of aloe vera, or I squeeze two bulbinella leaves over the area (*Bulbine frutescens*) or dilute 2 teaspoons of apple cider vinegar in 2 tablespoons of water and dab on frequently.

USING AROMATIC LAVENDER OILS

LAVENDER COLOGNE

This is an old formula that was made in the sixteenth century:

8 drops lavender essential oil
4 drops bergamot essential oil
3 drops clove essential oil
2 drops rose essential oil
4 teaspoons vodka
2 teaspoons distilled water

Drop the oils into a 30 ml glass bottle, add the vodka, seal and shake well. After 48 hours add the distilled

water and shake. Leave to mature for a month in a cool dark place, then test it on the inside of your wrist and if there is no reaction, then use lavishly.

LAVENDER MOSQUITO AND FLY REPELLENT

Using your own essential oil, this wonderfully fragrant creamy lotion can be rubbed onto chair legs, or a little lightly dabbed onto pillows – it is washable. It is best to rub it onto feet and forearms, but only if you've tested it on the inside of your wrist to see if your skin is sensitive or not.

4 teaspoons lavender essential oil
2 teaspoons eucalyptus essential oil
6 teaspoons apple cider vinegar
2 tablespoons good aqueous cream

Mix everything together vigorously. Spoon into a sterilised screw-top jar and label.

THE BEDTIME HERB

Lavender oil is a beautiful oil that will help your sleep pattern restore itself. Aromatherapists call lavender oil 'the harmonising oil', because it helps you to switch off and let go of all the rush and flurry of events in a busy day. My grandmother suggested a gentle walk along the rows of lavender before getting ready for bed. It has been my experience through some very difficult and upsetting times, that walking in the garden at night helped me to calm down, and crushing the lavenders in my hands as I strolled and smelled them, deeply inhaling the scent, certainly calmed, soothed and restored me. It helped me to start the forgiveness process. This is why a little pillow filled with fresh lavender is so comforting.

I am never without my little bottle of lavender essential oil. A drop or two on a tissue or handkerchief, which you smell frequently, will help you to calm down if you can't walk in the gardens at night, or if your little lavender pillow can't be filled with fresh sprigs.

LAVENDER SLEEP INDUCER

6-10 drops lavender essential oil
a small bunch of lavender

Drop lavender essential oil onto the bunch of fresh lavender. Massage the flowers and leaves gently to release and mingle their oils with the essential oils. Fold a large handkerchief around the bunch of lavender and tuck it under your pillow, or make a small pillowcase of cotton – about 30 x 24 cm – and stuff the bunch of fragrant lavender into it and tuck it under your pillow. All through the night, not only will your whole bed be scented by the little pillow, but your hands will be too, once you've softened the leaves and flowers in your hands. You will unravel, you will start to relax, and your restless mind will calm and quieten … sweet dreams!

LAVENDER BURNER OF SIMMERING POTPOURRI

This is a fabulous room freshener. It is also good for calming you down and helping you to unwind. Not only will the burner impart the wonderful fragrance of lavender on the room, it will also fill it with lavender's deodorising, antiseptic, antibacterial and antiviral properties. So it will keep the air healthy, especially in a sick room, or if someone has flu or a cold. It will also dissipate the smell of tobacco, pets and cooking smells.

1 cup dried lavender flowers (L. intermedia var.
   'Grosso', or L. intermedia 'Margaret Roberts' or
   L. latifolia 'Grandmother's lavender')
1 teaspoon essential oil and 4 teaspoons potpourri oil
   mixed
1 tablespoon crushed cinnamon sticks (not powder)
2 teaspoons of crushed cloves (not powder)

Mix the one teaspoon of essential lavender oil with the 3 teaspoons of lavender potpourri oil. Add to the spices and mix well. Store in a screw-top jar overnight. Add another 2 teaspoons of lavender potpourri oil to the dried lavender flowers and spoon into a large jar and shake well. The next day mix the spice mix into the lavender flowers and shake up. Seal for a week and give it a daily shake.

In a burner – a small pot warmed by a candle held in a pottery glow pot – mix 1 tablespoon of the lavender mixture, headily fragrant by now and into the little top pot pour 2 tablespoons of water. Light the candle, and as the lavender-infused water begins to heat up from the candle flame, the room will fill with the memory-making scent of lavender fields. Top up every now and then with a little water to prevent it from drying out and burning. Wash the pot out and start afresh the next day.

This exquisite bedding, part of the Woolworths Margaret Roberts Lavender range, keeps the little lavender-filled Teddy bear company.

LAVENDER VAPOURISING RING

Once it was very fashionable to have a metal ring with a groove in it to hold lavender essential oil that fitted neatly over a light bulb on a bedside light. The warmth of the globe dissipated the fragrant oil and it filled the room, keeping insects away and freshening the air.

For many years I have made a ceramic ring of carefully fired porcelain onto which a little lavender oil can be dropped. The porcelain, which is unglazed, will quickly absorb the oil, and when it is warmed it will disperse it into the atmosphere. This is still one of our best sellers in the Herbal Centre shop. If it is used in a bedroom with lavender essential oil, it has a beautifully calming, sleep-inducing effect. If you do not have a vapourising ring, drop a little oil onto a light bulb – literally just a drop or two – before switching it on. Relax as the fragrance gently fills the room.

LAVENDER ESSENTIAL OIL BATH

This is a very precious recipe for a very particular bath. It is relaxing, calming and quieting. Keep it in a little bottle on the edge of the bath and add a little at a time to a steaming bath. It is potent, so add only a few drops at a time … then relax … add a few more drops … relax again. This is not an ordinary bath oil or bath mixture, but one that actually helps with anxiety and tension. It must be made with essential oil.

½ cup almond oil
½ cup grape-seed oil
2 teaspoons lavender essential oil
1 teaspoon rose essential oil
10 drops chamomile essential oil

Pour the almond oil and grape-seed oil into a glass jar, seal and shake. Add the lavender, rose and chamomile essential oils, and shake, shake, shake. Stand overnight – don't hurry this blend, it needs to react together, then shake, shake, shake. Very carefully pour the heady mixture into small glass bottles with good screw-top lids.

A little of this special oil goes a long way. Never add more than 10 ml at a time to the bath. So use those 10 millilitres drop by drop. I start off with about 10 drops, then as I lie back in the water, I add another 4 or 5 drops and so on, over a period of about 15 minutes. The oils will dissipate and you will feel so much better. Wash yourself languidly and gently with lavender soap. Wrap yourself in a big warm fluffy towel, find your softest silkiest pajamas and climb into bed in super-relaxed mode.

I have a cup of lavender tea just before I turn out the light – which, by the way, has a dab of lavender essential oil in a vapourising ring, which rests on the globe. You will be amazed at what this ritual does. You will even find yourself picking a bunch of fresh lavender to tuck under your pillow before you start your peaceful bath. It works! Store the other little bottles in a cool dark cupboard to await the next special-occasion relaxing bath. Keep out of reach of children.

Using lavender medicinally

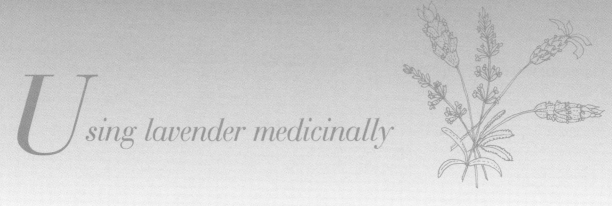

Important: Always consult your doctor before starting a home treatment.

Because of lavender's ancient proven uses, it appears in many natural remedies, often taken internally as a tea, or used externally as a compress or lotion, or in a massage cream or oil.

The earliest use I can remember was a fragrant soothing tea for headaches. Naturally, this was made with fresh lavender leaves and flowers. Medicinally it seems that L. intermedia var. 'Grosso' and L. intermedia var. 'Margaret Roberts' are the best lavenders to use and also if you can grow L. angustifolia. Europe uses this lavender medicinally:

STANDARD BREW TEA

This tea can be sipped to soothe a tension headache or lessen the effects of dizziness, nausea, anxiety, nervousness, nervous headache, muscular tension, indigestion, flatulence, bad breath, depression, sleeplessness and hyperactivity. Our grandmothers made it for rheumatic aches and pains, gout, arthritic joints, stiff muscles and leg cramps. I find myself taking the tea for insomnia, and wake the next morning free of the backache and cramps from the previous night. So, perhaps lavender's remarkable properties can be further scientifically validated as its centuries of use have established. Lavender has antiseptic, antibacterial, antifungal and analgesic properties and is also a gentle astringent and deep cleanser.

¼ cup fresh lavender leaves and flowers
1 cup boiling water
honey or lemon juice (optional)

Pour the boiling water over the fresh lavender leaves and flowers. Let it stand for 5 minutes Strain, and sweeten with a little honey if liked, or add a squeeze of lemon juice. It is delicious even on its own. Sip slowly.

LAVENDER LOTION

This simple soothing lotion is an excellent wash for sunburn, grazes, itchiness, rashes, infected cuts, mild burns and insect bites and stings.

2 cups fresh lavender leaves of (L. intermedia var. 'Margaret Roberts')
2½ litres water

Boil up the fresh lavender leaves in the water for 10 minutes. Set aside to cool, then strain. Use as a wash or dab on as a cleansing lotion. Keep the excess in the fridge. I use this fragrant brew in a spritz bottle or the bottle used for misting plants so that the fine spray can be a sunburn soother. Spray frequently to relieve the pain and heat. Lavender's analgesic properties come to fore here. It is very effective, even for small burns.

LAVENDER MASSAGE CREAM

I am never without this superb cream for aches, itches, cramps and sprains and it is wonderfully soothing massaged into aching heels and calf muscles after a long hike or into an aching neck and shoulders after a day's sport.

1 cup aqueous cream
1 cup lavender leaves and flowers (L. intermedia var. 'Margaret Roberts' or 'Grosso')
10 drops lavender essential oil
2 teaspoons wheatgerm oil

Warm the aqueous cream and lavender leaves and flowers gently together in a double boiler for 20 minutes. Strain out flowers and leaves. Add the lavender essential oil and wheatgerm oil. Mix well, pour into a sterilised screw-top jar and use lavishly.

LAVENDER COMPRESS

Do not underestimate the soothing qualities of lavender over a boil, bruise, sprain or aching joint.

soft tender little branches of lavender (Lavandula allardii var. 'African Pride' or L. allardii, Dutch lavender)
boiling water

Pick enough sprigs to cover the injured area. Cover the sprigs with boiling water and steep for 5 minutes or enough to thoroughly soften them. The big fragrant leaves of these lavenders soften beautifully in hot water. Scoop out the sprigs and apply wet and warm to the injured area. Cover with a towel and relax. I warm the towel by placing a hot-water bottle over it, supported by a pillow if necessary. Relax for 15 minutes.

NOTE: *Be careful to test if the lavender sprigs are comfortably warm before applying.*

LAVENDER STEAM INHALER

The misery of blocked sinuses, colds, 'flu and nasal congestion is greatly relieved by a lavender steam inhaler.

2 litres boiling water
6 sprigs lavender
6 drops eucalyptus oil
6 drops lavender oil

Pour the boiling water into a large basin over the lavender sprigs. Add the eucalyptus oil and the lavender oil. Make a tent with a towel over your head, and bend over the steaming bowl, inhale the steam, keeping your eyes closed. As a bonus your skin will feel soft and clean and the wrinkles will have disappeared, and you'll be breathing easier.

WARNING: *Do not do this steaming procedure if you have thread veins.*

LAVENDER STEAM CLEANSER

This steam treatment will help a spotty, greasy or problem skin enormously.

Bunch of lavender (L. allardii 'African Pride' or L. allardii Dutch Lavender)
Boiling water
6 drops lavender essential oil

Pick a bunch of lavender and cover it with boiling water. Add the lavender essential oil. Wash the face well and pat dry. Make a towel tent over your head, close your eyes and lower your face into the steam until it condenses on the skin. Pat dry and do not wash off for a while. If this treatment can be done once a week, it will make a big difference to the skin, refining and cleansing it as the strained cooled water makes an excellent lotion. Pour it into a plant mister and spray frequently over the face to keep oiliness at bay and to freshen the skin. The natural astringent abilities of the lavender works as a tonic refining the skin and closing the pores.

WARNING: *Do not use this steaming procedure if you have thread veins.*

The fragrant leaves and flowers of L. intermedia *'Margaret Roberts'.*

Lavender in the home and garden

The need to use truly natural products is now a serious issue. We need to look at natural insecticides, sprays and room fresheners before spraying more poisons into our already polluted environment. Companion planting is essential to eliminate the need for garden pesticides. Lavender fills this role admirably. Its strong oils are effective in chasing aphids, white fly, mildew, mice, rats, fleas and even fish moths.

I remember my grandmother placing sprigs and sachets of lavender richly scented with lavender oil, bought in small bottles from the corner chemist, under cupboards, behind bookshelves, into drawers and even tucked up behind the sofa and kitchen sink. Rats and mice hate the smell and small balls of cotton wool soaked in lavender oil and wiped along the skirting, window frames and door steps, will deter many a mouse who dares to enter. We never had a mouse, fish moth or fly in the house – they fled from the wonderful rich fragrance of the lavender.

LAVENDER TO ENHANCE YOUR HOME

LAVENDER POTPOURRI

This is my favourite recipe, and probably best seller, if you are lucky enough to find it in the shops. Use this potpourri to stuff coat-hangers and sachets and fill bags or pretty bowls tied with ribbons. I have a whole series of gift items made with this recipe: small sachets for the car, large sachets for the linen cupboard and flat sachets for behind books.

2 cups minced dried lemon peel
10 cups dried lavender stem, leaves and flowers (use any lavender, L. dentata is decorative and dries well and the little flower cones of the dentatas absorb the oils beautifully)
1 cup cloves
1 cup cinnamon and cassia pieces
1 cup coriander seeds
½ cup allspice berries
2 cups finely chopped lavender stems
a few little flowers which absorb the oils beautifully
2 tablespoons lavender oil (not the lavender essential oil used in aromatherapy, but a pleasant synthetic blend – a potpourri oil – bought from the chemist and easily available)

Mix the lemon peel with the cloves, cinnamon and cassia, coriander seeds, allspice berries and the lavender stems. Add the lavender oil. Tip everything into a large glass jar with a screw top. Shake daily and add more oil. Shake again. Leave to blend well, about 1 week, then add more oil and lavender leaves and flowers. Keep it lightly sealed and shake up daily for another week, adding more oil as needed.

LAVENDER ROOM SPRAY

I frequently make this spray up fresh. It helps to keep flies and mosquitoes away, and during the summer months seems to cool and freshen the room beautifully. During winter I leave the pot simmering on the stove gently all day, and open the interleading doors so that it can permeate the whole house. This is a lovely way of getting rid of stale cooking smells, pet smells and lingering tobacco smells. It also humidifies the air.

10 sprigs lavender leaves and flowers (L. allardii 'African Pride' or L. allardii Dutch lavender)
3 litres of water
a few drops lavender essential oil

Boil the sprigs of lavender, leaves and flowers in 3 litres water for 20 minutes. Cool, strain and discard the lavender. Add the lavender essential oil. Pour into a spritz bottle with a pump action and spray liberally and lavishly all over the room and all around while sitting out on the patio to keep mosquitoes away.

NOTE: *Lavender essential oil needs to be used for the room spray, as this is safe if it is inhaled in its mist-fine particles.*

REFRESHING LEMON AND LAVENDER ROOM SPRAY

I love this wonderfully air-cleansing and deodorising room spray, and keep it handy in the kitchen and the bathroom. I also spray the dogs' kennels, baskets, blankets and cushions, and lay everything out in the sun for a day every week, and this wonderful spray gets rid of all those smells. Incidentally and surprisingly, after regular use, there is no sign of a tick or a flea!

2 cups lavender flowers, stripped off their stems (any lavender, especially L. latifolia 'Grandmother's lavender' and L. allardii 'African Pride')
2 cups lemon grass leaves, roughly chopped, or lemon verbena leaves, or a mixture of both
½ cup whole cloves
½ cup coriander seeds
1 cup thinly pared lemon rind – no pith – that has been dried in the sun
2 cups cane spirit or vodka
1 cup distilled water
20 drops lavender essential oil
10 drops lemon oil

Mix the lavender flowers, lemon grass leaves, cloves, coriander seeds and lemon rind. Pour into a large glass jar with a screw-top lid. Add the cane spirit and shake, shake, shake. Keep the jar in a dark cupboard for 2 weeks. Give it a daily shake. Strain out herbs and spices and discard. Add the distilled water, the lavender essential oil and the lemon oil. Pour into a spritz bottle and shake, shake, shake and spray lavishly into cupboards and behind cupboards. Shake up every now and then to disperse oils.

LAVENDER AS A NATURAL INSECT REPELLENT

LAVENDER INCENSE

For an evening party, save all the lavender twigs and branches that the leaves have been stripped off. Clip and tie them into neat bundles with coarse string or raffia. Stand the twigs in an earthenware flowerpot filled with sand so that they don't fall over, then light them. I put a few drops of lavender oil into the bundle before the party so that they really smell wonderful. Placed out of the way, the gentle smouldering smoke chases mosquitoes and flies and gives a party atmosphere. Keep out of children's reach.

LAVENDER INSECT-REPELLING SPRAY

I use this insect-repelling spray particularly for aphids, mildew, rust and white fly on houseplants, vegetables and inside the dogs' kennels and baskets. The brew can be used to wash out birdcages, rabbit hutches, kennels and chicken nesting boxes.

½ *bucket lavender twigs, leaves and flowers, roughly chopped (L. allardii 'African Pride' and the stoechas lavenders)*
¼ *bucket mixed rue and khakibos or marigold sprigs roughly chopped*
1 *bucket boiling water*
1 *cup soap powder*

Pour boiling water over all the sprigs, leaves, twigs and flowers and let everything stand overnight to draw. Next morning strain, discard the lavender sprigs and flowers and mix the soap powder into the scented water. Splash or spray onto plants, or use as a wash for kennels, bird cages, etc.

LAVENDER INSECT-REPELLING CANDLES

Through the many years of candle-making, which began when my children were tiny, I found lavender to be the most soothing fragrance for their bedrooms. During those years there was no electricity on farms, so candles were tremendously important. I used combinations of citronella oil and lavender for midsummer when moths and mosquitoes were at their worst. Thirty years ago there were no varied and beautiful candles for sale like there are now. My simple method of candle-making is easy for anyone to follow, and candles always make welcome gifts.

In an old saucepan, melt down several ordinary cheap candles. I always used white, as it is easy to colour by merely adding a few scrapings from the children's wax crayons. Naturally I chose mauve, palest blue or deep purple. Once you have melted 6 candles add:
2 *teaspoons crayon scrapings*
2 *tablespoons lavender flowers and buds – those tiny little bits stripped off their stems (Lavandula intermedia var. 'Margaret Roberts' or 'Grosso')*
3 *teaspoons lavender potpourri oil*
1 *teaspoon citronella oil bought from your chemist*

Mix everything together in the pot and pour into paper cups or milk cartons in which you have fixed a wick. Don't use polystyrene cups as they will melt. Wicks can be bought at craft shops. Plait 3 wicks from the candles you melted down, by knotting the end through a hole in the carton. Seal with masking tape underneath, and tie the other end to a pencil that you have placed across the top. The plaiting makes a more substantial wick – plait tightly, and allow the wax to set. Top up with more wax as a dimple is often left near the wick. Peel away the paper once it is set, and trim off any rough spots with a sharp knife. Once you light the candle, add the odd drop of lavender oil to the melted wax under the flame. Stand the candle in a sturdy saucer or container so that it does not topple over. Always protect your candles and keep out of the reach of children.

For a party table make several small candles. Stand them in a shallow water-filled glass dish with masses of lavender flowers all around them. The whole room will be scented with not a mosquito or fly in sight!

LAVENDER SNAIL REPELLENT

all the eggshells you can collect
½ cup dried lavender flowers, stripped off their stems,
for every cup of crushed eggshells (Lavandula
intermedia var. 'Margaret Roberts' or 'Grosso', or
L. latifolia 'Grandmother's lavender')

Place the eggshells on a large baking tray and 'bake' for 10 minutes at 180 °C. This is to facilitate the crushing of the shells. Add the lavender flowers, mix well and sprinkle along the paths and under the plants that the snails love. Make little circles of the lavender and eggshells around lettuces. When the snails cross the eggshell-and-lavender trail, it will stick to their slimy bodies and they literally curl up and die peacefully.

LAVENDER TO NEUTRALISE SMELLS

A KITCHEN CANDLE

A kitchen candle is a wonderful idea for neutralising kitchen odours.

home-made candle wax (see 'lavender insect-repelling
candles' above for method)
wick
long lavender flowers
lavender potpourri oil
clove oil

Select a glass tumbler, and secure a wick by attaching it to the bottom of the glass with a blob of putty, Prestik or thick candle wax. Tie the top of the wick to a pencil, which you have placed across the top of the glass and gently pour in the wax and press long lavender flowers down the side of the glass as the wax cools. Add more drops of lavender potpourri oil and clove oil as the candle cools. Clove oil also has deodorising qualities. Both clove oil and lavender potpourri oil can be bought from the chemist. Burn the candle in the kitchen when you're cooking cabbage, cauliflower, fish, or when you are pickling to remove the smells. Carefully add drops of lavender and clove oil to the top of the candle as it burns, but never onto the flame.

AIR FRESHENER BOWL

This is a wonderful gift for both kitchen and bathroom, and it gets rid of all those old musty smells, cooking smells, smoking smells and even old dog smells. It is also quick and easy to make.

2 cups coarse salt
½ cup cloves
½ cup coriander seeds
½ cup cinnamon pieces
2 cups dried lavender flowers, stripped off their stems
1 cup minced lemon rind, dried in the sun until hard
lavender potpourri oil

Mix the salt, cloves, coriander seeds and cinnamon pieces. Lightly crush in a pestle and mortar, then add dried lavender flowers and lemon rind, and mix thoroughly. Pour into a large screw-top jar. Add 3 teaspoons lavender potpourri oil and shake, shake, shake. Leave in a dark cupboard for 10 days, giving it a daily shake. Add another 2–3 teaspoons of the potpourri oil, shake up well and leave overnight. Next morning spoon into bowls, and place in the bathroom, toilet, kitchen, and in the cupboards. Enjoy the scent! Revive from time to time by adding more potpourri oil and shake it up.

NOTE: *If you live at the coast leave the salt out and substitute it with extra dried lemon peel, and an extra ½ cup of cloves.*

Lavender candles bring a soothing fragrance to the bedroom and a deodorising effect to the bathroom.

LAVENDER TO PROTECT YOUR FURNITURE

This old-fashioned lavender furniture polish is part of my memory bank. Its evocative scent takes me back to my Gordon's Bay childhood with my grandmother. It brings back the scent in the sea cottage, not only of lavender drying or in sachets, but also the strong scent of antique furniture being lovingly polished. I made this furniture polish as a young bride living on an isolated farm and I make it today at the drop of a hat. The furniture literally gleams with pleasure as the wood soaks it up.

10 cups fresh lavender flowers
1 cup beeswax (ask a friendly beekeeper to keep some aside)
2 teaspoons lavender potpourri oil
4 cups linseed oil

Pound and crush the lavender flowers lightly. In a double boiler simmer the beeswax and the crushed lavender flowers, pushing them down so that the wax coats them. Gradually and very slowly add the linseed oil, stirring all the time. Let it simmer for 5 minutes, then stand for 10 minutes off the heat. Strain and discard the lavender flowers. Add the potpourri oil and mix everything together well. Pour into tins or wide-mouthed glass jars and seal.

To use your lavender polish rub a soft cloth gently over the surface and then rub over the furniture. Leave it to rest for an hour, then buff up with a fresh soft cloth and plenty of elbow grease.

NOTES *A little beeswax goes a long way. Any lavender is fine to use, but I love* L. latifolia *'Grandmother's lavender' best, because she used this to make the furniture polish.*
Linseed oil will darken wood. If you have light woods, make the polish by substituting pale olive oil for the linseed oil.

Lavender gifts

This is my favourite way of using lavender – as a fragrant bath and bedroom relaxant and for making a glorious array of scented gifts and treasures that will be cherished for years to come. This is where you can be at your most creative, and this is where you will make your creativity pay. Everyone loves lavender, especially these lavender gift lines and beauty products. I have never been able to keep up with the demand.

Our huge Herbal Centre shop has more lavender products than any other lines, and we are forever creating new items to satisfy the demand, which shows no sign of abating. Try your hand at these special items. A gift made and given with love – what could be more rewarding?

LAVENDER LIQUEUR

This is one of the most unusual and fascinating gifts and is suitable for men, especially the man who has everything, this is one gift he won't have! And he won't be able to wait to try it out!

Traditionally Lavender Liqueur was taken in a little hot water to ease the symptoms of a cold, but in France where this liqueur originated, made by the monks using brandy or wine, it was taken as an after-dinner digestive and given as a calming medicine.

Lavender liqueur became popular again in the eighteenth century where it graced many a public inn, and was served at the end of a feast with aniseed added to aid the digestion.

2 cups vodka
2 cups white sugar

4 tablespoons fresh lavender flowers (Lavandula intermedia var. 'Grosso' is the one most favoured for the best flavour, but experiment with others)
2 tablespoons fresh lemon balm leaves (Melissa officinalis)
1 teaspoon lemon zest – pare off zest carefully so as no to have any pith

Place the vodka and the sugar in a double boiler and warm until dissolved, about 5 minutes. Add the lavender flowers, lemon balm and lemon zest, and stir for 2 minutes over the simmering water. Cover the pot and remove from the stove. Leave it to infuse over the water overnight. Next morning strain through a muslin-lined sieve. Pour into a sterilised glass bottle and cork well. Leave in a dark cupboard for 2 months before drinking. Serve in a tiny liqueur glass with a sprig of fresh lavender flowers. Suggest to your guests that they stir the liqueur with the lavender before sipping it very slowly.

LAVENDER MARMALADE

Once you have tried the fresh lavender fragrance in this delicious marmalade, you will never go back to ordinary marmalade. Lavender lends itself admirably to citrus products. It's a wonderful gift that everyone enjoys and, by the way, is sought after by restaurants!

FILLS 2–4 JARS, DEPENDING ON THE SIZE OF THE JARS
6 oranges
2 large lemons
sprig of lavender and fresh lavender flowers (use Lavandula intermedia var. 'Margaret Roberts' or 'Grosso')
water – about 2–3 cups
3 kg sugar

Thinly slice the fruit, removing all the pips and thick pieces of skin. Place the pips with a sprig of lavender in a little bag. Place the oranges, water and pips into a large heavy-bottomed saucepan. Simmer for about 1 hour. Remove the little bag of pips and add 2 tablespoons lavender flowers. Gradually add the sugar, stirring all the time, then simmer for another hour or until setting point. Stir occasionally. Remove from stove and let stand for 10-15 minutes. Pour into hot sterilised jars, seal and label. Tie a pretty mauve ribbon around the bottle, and, with a sprig or two of fresh lavender flowers tucked into it, it makes a beautiful gift.

POTPOURRI WITH LAVENDER AND PURPLE FLOWERS

This is a different potpourri that is very spectacular in an open bowl – not only for its lavender variations, but for its other mauve and purple flowers. It needs to be made in spring to catch all the flowers at their best.

10 cups mixed lavender flowers (I use them all: the French and Spanish lavenders as well as the intermedias and even the fern-leaf lavenders)
3 cups wisteria flowers
2-3 cups petrea flowers
3-4 cups sea lavender (Statice perezii – this statice is so called because it grows easily near the sea)
1-2 cups Salvia leucantha flowers
1-2 cups heliotrope flowers

You can substitute any of these for what you have, for example purple sweet-peas, or any of the statice varieties that are in shades of mauve and purple, pressed purple pansies – press the flowers in an old telephone book. The ratio is ideally half lavender and half the rest of the purple flowers altogether, giving around 20 cups in all.

Fixative

The fixative is made from dried lemon, orange and naartjie peel. You will need 4 cups, and it is to this that the fragrant potpourri oil is added. Mince the fresh peels and spread out on trays to dry in the sun, turning every now and then. Dry everything else on newspaper in the shade and give it a daily turn. Keep everything separate as the different flowers all take different times to dry.

Once the flowers are all dry, mix them together with a light hand as you don't want to break or spoil the delicate flowers. Add at least 6 teaspoons of lavender potpourri oil to the dried peels and mix together in a large-mouthed jar or container, like a crock. I use a large deep baking dish with a good tight-fitting lid.

Add to this the spices – this is also part of the fixative:
1 cup cloves
2 cups cinnamon or cassia pieces broken into small bits
2 cups coriander seeds
1 cup star anise

Mix these together and add to the peel. Add more lavender potpourri oil and mix well. Seal. Give it a shake once or twice a day for 10 days. Then mix gently into the flowers. Seal, and give it another 10 days to mature. During that time add more lavender potpourri oil if needed, and finally pack into pretty bowls or baskets and add the pressed pansies to decorate this breathtaking bowl. This is a very showy potpourri, and you will be thrilled with its scent and the look of all the shades of mauve and purple.

KEEPING YOUR POTPOURRI IN TIP-TOP CONDITION

If your potpourri is a gift enclose this tip beautifully handwritten or printed on hand-made paper.

Cover bowl at night with a flat glass disc cut to the size of the bowl, but 1 cm larger all round. This acts as a sealer and keeps the scent in and dust out. Remove the glass disc when you are in the room and stand the bowl on it. Revive the potpourri from time to time with a few drops of lavender oil dropped into the very centre of the bowl – make a little well inside it. You will see that all the peel and spices have settled down there; this is where you drop the oil in.

Give the bowl an instant lift by adding fresh petrea flowers. These dry quickly and hold their colour well.

SHOE SACHET DEODORISER

This easy-to-make little gift is a sure seller in our Herbal Centre shop, it is much loved by old and young alike. You tuck the elongated sachet into your shoes, specially your running shoes, at night. The deodorising abilities of lavender and cloves freshen the shoes up beautifully and your cupboard smells good and clean and fresh!

1½ cups dried lavender flowers (L. intermedia var. 'Margaret Roberts', 'Grosso' or L. latifolia 'Grandmother' lavender).
¾ cup cloves
½ cup cinnamon broken into small pieces
¾ cup dried minced lemon peel
about 4 teaspoons lavender potpourri oil

Add the oil to the cinnamon, cloves and lemon peel. Mix in a screw-top jar and leave to saturate for at least 4 days. Give it a good daily shake. Then mix in the lavender and store for 2 more days. Shake up well. Make 2 sachets 6 cm wide x 15 cm long out of mauve poplin or cotton. Leave one end open and stitch securely, and make a small hem at the open end. Turn inside out and fill with the fragrant lavender mixture.

Tie tightly at the top with a ribbon and, if it is for a gift, package in a cellophane bag that you can seal well.

When it is not in use store in the cellophane bag to keep the scent. Revive every now and then by shaking out all the lavender mixture into a bowl, and add more lavender potpourri oil – about 4 teaspoons and mix well and store in a glass screw-top jar for at least 4 days so that it can infuse well. Give it a daily shake and then re-stuff your shoe sachets.

NOTE *When you make sachets of any kind, always let the mixture mature with the potpourri oil in it before filling the bags, and shake up thoroughly daily. In this way you won't get oil spots on the sachet material.*

LAVENDER PEACE PILLOW

This is the perfect gift for insomniacs, I must have made thousands of these over the years and they have been taken all over the world as travel pillows. The size I like best is 40 x 25 cm – that is to my mind the most comfortable.

Make an inner pillow of pure cotton. Stuff with foam chips or a polyester fibre filler. Make a small flat sachet 18 x 12 cm and fill with this mixture:
1 cup dried lavender flowers (Lavandula intermedia var. 'Margaret Roberts' or 'Grosso') stripped off their stems
1 cup dried lavender leaves (I find my Grandmother's lavender best – it has the longest-lasting smell)
½ cup cloves
½ cup chopped dried lemon peel
lavender potpourri oil

Mix the lemon peel and cloves, add 1 tablespoon lavender oil. Keep sealed in a screw-top bottle. Give it a daily shake. After 1 week add the dried lavender leaves and flowers. Add a little more oil and keep sealed for a further week, and shake up daily. Fill the small flat sachet with this fragrant blend and sew up the end. Tuck this into the centre of the pillow surrounded by the stuffing, and sew the end of the pillow closed.

Although we have reached the end of this small lavender journey; it really is only the beginning of a fascination that will never leave you and the journey ahead will never fully be completed, I sincerely hope. I love the thought that in this great Labiatae family to which lavender belongs, cross-pollination is something that happens fairly easily; and with that profound thought in mind I look earnestly and carefully for any new variances in the fluttering and high hope that a new breathtaking beauty will emerge, and it's happening right now all over the world!

In the language of flowers lavender means devotion – I easily identify with that, and my hope is that you will feel it too, and that lavender will become etched into your soul the way it is in mine, and that your garden of lavender will give you much pleasure always.

Lavender means devotion,
A sincere and dear emotion
It's loved by all,
It's growing tall,
It's turned into a potion
And a soothing healing lotion!

Come share the scent, the look, the taste,
And get to know this plant in haste.
And in its fragrant mauve invest.
We know that lavender is best
To quiet and calm and give us rest,
And leave us feeling we are blessed.

So up and planting we must go
And water well each precious row,
Expand and nurture our mauve field,
And count the bunches, sales and yields,
Rejoicing in its easy growing.
It's thoughts, ideas and more we're sowing,
Creating, making, doing and giving,
Lavender makes our life worth living!

Index